Family Dinners

HOW TO FEED YOUR KIDS AND GET
THEM TALKING AT THE TABLE

JANET PETERSON

Gibbs Smith, Publisher
Salt Lake City

To my family, for the joy each one brings to the dinner table:
Larry, Scott, Anna, Andrew, Emily, Isabella, Stephanie, David,
Brinley, Ben, Amanda, Emma, Tom, Megan, Alex, Sophia, Greg,
Audrey, Jeff, Vicky, and Brent

First Edition
10 09 08 07 06   5 4 3 2 1

Text © 2006 Janet Peterson

Published by
Gibbs Smith, Publisher
P. O. Box 667
Layton, Utah 84041

Orders: 1.800.748.5439
www.gibbs-smith.com

Designed by Sheryl Dickert
Printed and bound in Canada

Library of Congress Cataloging-in-Publication Data
Peterson, Janet.
  Family dinners : easy ways to feed your kids and get them talking at the table / Janet Peterson.—1st ed.
    p. cm.
  ISBN 1-58685-764-9
  1. Dinners and dining. I. Title.

TX737.P43 2006
641.5'4—dc22

2005027274

Contents

Acknowledgments

Jennifer Grillone, my editor at Gibbs Smith, Publisher, has skillfully and enthusiastically guided this cookbook from inception to publication. Working with her has been one of the joys of creating *Family Dinners*.

I wish to thank the many good cooks from coast to coast whose recipes have been adapted for *Family Dinners*. In particular, heartfelt thanks go to dear friends Betty Draper, Nancy Hughes, Pat Menlove, and Kathryn Wade, and the members of the "Gone to Pieces" quilt group.

My loving husband, Larry, not only cheerfully served as the official taster but also encouraged me throughout the process and provided me with my dream test kitchen.

Introduction

Families, no matter their size or makeup, must be fed daily. Because dinner comes around every 24 hours, it's a perfect opportunity to bring your family together. Although going out to dinner as a family can be fun and memorable, many of life's best lessons are learned at home around the kitchen table. It's a time to talk and laugh, share thoughts and ideas, try new recipes and enjoy old favorites, build traditions and make memories. Family dinners are also a time for family members to discuss issues, socialize, express love, and fortify relationships in a myriad of other ways. Families who eat together regularly provide a sense of security and emotional well-being to their children, and parents are able to instill values and beliefs that are important to them.

Make It Simple

Cooking dinner doesn't need to be a time-consuming production. Food does not have to be elaborate to be good nor do you have to spend hours in the kitchen to be a good cook. Simple recipes prepared quickly can yield great meals. This book offers an abundance of recipes that are easy to make and taste great. Planning ahead and having a well-stocked pantry and refrigerator can eliminate that end of day frustration about "What's for dinner?"

Cooking is a skill which is simply not that difficult. If you can read a cookbook and have a willingness to try, you can learn to be a good cook. A little time, an adventurous attitude, and some to attention to detail make it that much easier. Resources for finding recipes and improving cooking skills are almost endless, including Internet sites, published cookbooks, newspapers, magazines, classes, television cooking shows, other cooks, family members, and friends. Cooking is a lifelong learning venture! It doesn't require perfection, but it can be improved along the way. Both novice and seasoned cooks alike can produce wonderful, healthy meals. Let all the family members help with family dinners, from shopping and food prep, to setting the table and washing the dishes. This book includes many tips and ideas on including children in helping with family meals.

Make It Fun

In addition to great recipes, Family Dinners offers dozens of tips and advice on bringing your family together at the table, including ideas for getting children involved, lively dinner conversations, and starting family traditions. Remember that an upbeat, pleasant atmosphere at the dinner table is as important as the food. Don't use dinnertime to resolve difficulties or cross-examine your kids about missed homework assignments or neglected chores. Instead enjoy each other's company and focus on the positive.

Make It a Priority

Families for whom eating dinner together regularly is a high priority in their lives can make it happen. Most people find time for things that really matter to them. Once gathering the family for dinner is recognized as important, you can find ways to include it in your schedule. While it may not be possible for your family to meet every single night around the table, you can improve the frequency of family dinners at home. Attitude, encouragement, invitation (and sometimes insistence) can bring families together more often at mealtime. There is no magic dinner hour. Be willing to be flexible in scheduling to get as many members of the family together for dinner as possible, whether it is as early as 4:30 p.m. or as late as 9:30 p.m.

Reap the Benefits

Children who grow up eating dinner with their families are simply better off than those who do not. Not only are they better nourished physically and have significantly better health than kids who eat a lot of fast food, the psychologically and emotional benefits can't be overstated either. Children learn social and conversational skills around the dinner table and develop a much stronger sense of self-worth and belonging than when they are left on their own for meals. Everyone needs to feel a sense of security, love, and connection.

In separate studies of teens conducted by Cincinnati Children's Hospital and the American Psychological Association, researchers concluded that youth who ate dinner with their families at least five times a week were less likely to smoke, drink, take drugs, have premarital sex, suffer depression, and break the law. So great is the power of family dinners upon teens' behavior that the National Center on Addiction and Substance Abuse (CASA) at Columbia University, launched an annual event, "Family Day—A Day to Eat Dinner with Your Children" to "to highlight the importance of parental involvement and encourage Americans to make family dinners a regular feature of their lives."

Conclusion

"Getting back to the table allows us to love and nurture each other and renew connections to our families. . . ." said Art Smith, personal chef for Oprah Winfrey. "Such connections are crucial in a fast-paced world where we feel more disconnected every day. One of the best ways I know to restore that daily balance is to sit down at the table."

Whether you are part of a big family or a small one, have kids at home or are an empty nester, or have one parent or two to help with meals, dinnertime is a great way to bring your family together to nurture and strengthen relationships. *Family Dinners* provides 300 quality recipes that are easy to prepare and taste great! The effort spent in preparing healthful and tasty meals and then gathering the family around the table to enjoy them together is one of the best investments any family can make.

Soups

CHICKEN NOODLE SOUP

Hot chicken soup really is a curative!

8	cups chicken stock or broth (low sodium)
3	carrots, thinly sliced
2	stalks celery, thinly sliced
¼	teaspoon black pepper
2	cups diced, cooked chicken
1	cup uncooked egg noodles
1	tablespoon snipped fresh dill weed or 1 teaspoon dried dill weed
1	tablespoon minced fresh parsley
	Salt to taste

In a large soup pot, bring stock or broth to a boil. Add carrots, celery, and pepper. Reduce heat and simmer, uncovered, 10 minutes. Add chicken and noodles; simmer until noodles are tender, about 8 minutes. Add dill, parsley, and salt, if desired. Cook another 5 minutes.

Serves 4

Save Time: When you don't have time to make your own stock, use bouillon granules or cubes, or canned chicken or beef broth.

CHICKEN AND WILD RICE SOUP

The aroma of soup simmering on the stove draws family members to the kitchen.

1	package (6 ounces) Uncle Ben's Long Grain & Wild Rice
1	small onion, chopped
2 to 3	carrots, sliced
3 to 4	stalks celery, sliced
3	cans (14 ounces each) chicken broth
⅓	cup butter
⅓	cup flour
½	teaspoon salt
½	teaspoon pepper
2	cups milk or half-and-half
1 to 2	chicken breasts, cooked and cubed
4 to 6	slices bacon, cooked and crumbled

Cook rice according to package directions and set aside. In a large soup pot or saucepan, cook onion, carrots, and celery in chicken broth until tender. In a medium saucepan, melt butter and add flour, stirring until a smooth paste is formed. Add salt and pepper. Slowly add milk, stirring constantly until sauce is thickened.

Add white sauce to pot with broth and vegetables, stirring until smooth. Add chicken and rice. Cook until soup is hot, but not boiling. Add bacon just before serving.

Serves 4 to 6

Serve this soup in a pretty or whimsical soup tureen.

4	slices bacon, diced
1	medium onion, chopped
1	small green pepper, chopped
1½	cups diced cooked ham
1	can (14 ounces) beef broth
1	quart water
1	large or 2 medium carrots, sliced
1	tablespoon soy sauce
1	can (14½ ounces) diced tomatoes
¼	teaspoon pepper
1½ to 2	cups frozen mixed vegetables
1	zucchini, sliced

In a large soup pot, cook bacon until crisp; remove from pan and drain on a paper towel. Pour out all but 1 tablespoon bacon grease. Sauté onion and green pepper in bacon grease until onion is soft. Return bacon to pan and add ham, beef broth, water, carrot, soy sauce, tomatoes, and pepper. Simmer for 1 hour. Add mixed vegetables and zucchini. Simmer another 30 minutes.

Serves 4 to 6

Family Tip: Once a week assign different family members various parts of dinner to prepare. One person could prepare the salad, another the vegetables, another the main course, and another the dessert. Allow family members to collaborate on the menu or to make it potluck.

BEAN AND BACON SOUP

During the school year, have a once-a-week Soup Night and audition new recipes.

1	tablespoon butter or margarine
1	small onion, chopped
4 to 6	slices bacon, cooked and diced
1	can (10¾ ounces) cream of mushroom soup
1	can (10¾ ounces) vegetarian vegetable soup
1	can (10¾ ounces) bean and bacon soup
1	cup frozen corn
1½	cups milk
½	cup water
2	potatoes, peeled, cooked, and diced
	Salt and pepper to taste

In a soup pot or large heavy saucepan, melt butter or margarine and cook onion until softened. Add bacon, cream of mushroom soup, vegetable soup, bean and bacon soup, corn, milk, water, and potatoes. Season to taste with salt and pepper. Cook over medium heat about 10 minutes until thoroughly heated. Stir often to prevent soup from sticking to pan.

Serves 6 to 8

Save Time: Read recipes before beginning preparation to gather equipment and ingredients, and to understand directions and time needed.

HEARTY BEAN SOUP

Collect interesting soup mugs in your travels and serve soup to your family in them.

1½ to 2	cups dried navy or Great Northern beans
	Water
4	cans (14 ounces each) or 2 quarts chicken broth
2	tablespoons fresh parsley, minced
2	bay leaves
½	teaspoon pepper
1	large onion, chopped
2	large carrots, sliced
2	celery stalks, sliced
	Salt to taste
6 to 8	pieces of bacon, cooked and crumbled

Put beans in a large soup pot or Dutch oven, then add enough water to cover by two inches. Bring to a boil and boil for 5 minutes. Turn off heat; cover and let stand for 2 hours. Drain liquid from beans.

To the beans, add chicken broth, parsley, bay leaves, pepper, and onion. Bring to a boil. Reduce heat and simmer for 1½ hours, or until beans are tender. Add carrots and celery; add more chicken broth or water, if needed. Add salt to taste. Cover and simmer for 25 to 30 minutes, until vegetables are tender. Add bacon. Remove bay leaves before serving.

Serves 8 to 10

Save Time: When short on time to make tomato soup, doctor canned tomato or vegetable soup by substituting V-8 juice for the water.

BLACK BEAN SOUP

Served cold, this makes a delicious black bean dip.

1	medium onion, chopped
2	cloves garlic, minced
1	tablespoon olive oil
3	cans (15 ounces each) black beans, rinsed and drained
2	cans (14½ ounces each) vegetable broth
2	handfuls Italian (flat leaf) parsley, minced
1	can (10 ounces) diced tomatoes and green chiles, undrained*
12	baby carrots
1	teaspoon cumin
½	teaspoon garlic salt
	Sour cream (optional)
	Minced fresh cilantro (optional)
	Tortilla chips (optional)

In a large saucepan or soup pot, sauté onion and garlic in oil for
2 to 3 minutes, until tender. Add black beans, vegetable broth, parsley,
tomatoes and green chiles, carrots, cumin, and garlic salt. Cook over
medium heat until carrots are tender. Remove from heat. Pour soup, in
portions, into a blender or food processor and process until smooth.
Return to soup pan and heat through. Serve with sour cream, cilantro,
and tortilla chips, if desired.

Serves 4 to 6

*Note: If you want the soup to be a little less spicy, do not use the entire
can of tomatoes and chiles.

BURGUNDY BEAN SOUP

Dress up canned Bean and Bacon Soup with this recipe.

- 2   cans (11½ ounces each) bean and bacon soup
- 1   can (10½ ounces) condensed beef broth
- 1   teaspoon instant minced onion
- 1   teaspoon Worcestershire sauce
- 2   cups water
- ½   cup cranberry or grape juice
  Pepper (optional)

In a large sauce pan, mix bean and bacon soup, beef broth, onion, Worcestershire sauce, water, and cranberry or grape juice. Bring to a boil, reduce heat, and cook for 15 minutes, stirring occasionally. Season with pepper, if desired.

Serves 4 to 6

CARROT LEEK SOUP

Just seeing this pretty orange-colored soup whets the appetite.

- 5   cups chicken broth (low sodium)
- 2   cups diced yams, or sweet or white potatoes
- 1½ cups sliced carrots
- 3   leeks, peeled and sliced
- 1   cup half-and-half or milk
- 1   cup sour cream (use low-fat if desired)
- 1   teaspoon salt, or to taste
  Freshly ground pepper

In a large soup pot or Dutch oven, combine chicken broth, yams or potatoes, carrots, and leeks. Cook until vegetables are tender. Put in a food processor or blender in portions and blend until smooth. Return to pot and add half-and-half or milk and sour cream. Season with salt and pepper to taste. Heat through but do not boil.

Serves 6

PASTA FAGIOLI

Pasta and beans in a tomato broth—molto bene! *Serve with crusty bread and a green salad.*

1	onion, chopped
2	cloves garlic, minced
1	stalk celery, sliced
1	carrot, sliced
2	tablespoons olive oil
2	cans (8 ounces each) tomato sauce
1	can (14 ounces) diced tomatoes
1	can (15 ounces) cannellini (white kidney) beans, rinsed and drained
1	can (15 ounces) navy or Great Northern beans, rinsed and drained
4	cups chicken broth or water
1	teaspoon salt
1½ to 2	teaspoons Italian seasoning
1	tablespoon dried parsley
1	bay leaf
⅓	cup grated Parmesan cheese + more for garnish
1	cup diced ham (optional)
¾	cup shell or small elbow macaroni (or other small pasta, such as ditalini)
	Freshly ground pepper (optional)

In a large soup pot or saucepan, sauté onion, garlic, celery, and carrot in olive oil until soft. Add tomato sauce, tomatoes, cannellini beans, navy or Great Northern beans, chicken broth or water, salt, Italian seasoning, parsley, bay leaf, Parmesan cheese, and ham, if desired. Bring to a boil and simmer, covered, for 30 minutes.

While soup is simmering, cook pasta in a separate saucepan in lightly salted water according to package directions until al dente. Drain and add to soup. Serve soup sprinkled with grated Parmesan cheese and freshly ground pepper, if desired.

Serves 6 to 8

SPLIT PEA SOUP

Serve this soup with a variety of crackers, cheeses, and fresh fruit.

1	package (16 ounces) split peas
1 or 2	ham hocks
1	large onion, diced
2	stalks celery, diced
1	large carrot, grated
1	tablespoon cider vinegar
2 to 3	tablespoons minced parsley
½ to 2	teaspoons garlic salt
	Freshly ground black pepper

Put split peas, ham hocks, and onion in a large saucepan or soup pot. Add water according to package directions on split peas. Simmer an hour or more. Add celery, carrot, vinegar, parsley, garlic salt, and pepper. Cook until desired consistency and softness of peas is reached (may take up to 4 hours). Remove ham hocks from soup. Cut bite-size ham pieces from bone and return to soup. Discard bones.

If reheating leftover soup, add more water as soup thickens as it cools.

Serves 8 to 10

Family Tip: Make laughter your favorite dinner recipe. Tell legendary family stories or recount the day's more humorous experiences (even experiences that were not humorous earlier in the day can bring on loads of laughter a few hours later).

CORN CHOWDER

Chowder is usually made with seafood; this is an "inland"
version with corn instead.

6	slices bacon, cooked and crumbled
1	small onion, chopped
2	cans (14¾ ounces each) cream-style corn
2	cups peeled, cubed potatoes, cooked
⅔	cup milk or light cream
2⅓	cups hot water (use water drained from potatoes)
1	teaspoon salt
¼	teaspoon garlic salt
1 to 1½	cups grated Swiss or cheddar cheese

In a large soup pot, cook bacon until crisp. Place cooked bacon on a
paper towel to drain. Drain grease from pot, leaving a little to sauté
onion. Cook onion in bacon grease until soft. Crumble bacon and return
it to pot. Add corn, cooked potatoes, milk or cream, water, salt, and garlic salt. Heat to simmer. Add cheese; stir until cheese is melted and
soup is thoroughly heated.

Serves 6 to 8

*Cooking Tip: Use instant potatoes to thicken soups
and stews.*

BAKED POTATO SOUP

This soup is oh so good on a cold winter's night.

4	large baking potatoes
½	cup butter
½	cup flour
6	cups milk
1½	teaspoons salt, or to taste
1	teaspoon white pepper
4	green onions, sliced
8	slices bacon, cooked and crumbled
1½	cups grated cheddar cheese
½	cup sour cream

Heat oven to 350° F.

Bake potatoes about 45 minutes, until soft when pierced with a fork. Cut potatoes in half and scoop out most of the centers into a bowl. In a soup pot or large saucepan, melt butter over low heat. Add flour, stirring until smooth. Cook mixture a minute longer, then gradually add milk, stirring constantly until thickened. Add potatoes, salt, pepper, green onions, bacon, and cheese. Simmer about 10 minutes. Add sour cream just before serving. Stir until heated through, but do not boil.

Serves 6 to 8

CREAM OF TOMATO SOUP

Only slightly more work than opening a can of tomato soup, this recipe is much tastier.

- ¼ cup butter
- ¼ cup flour
- 1 teaspoon salt
- 3 cups milk
- 4 cups tomato juice
- 1 teaspoon sugar
- 1 teaspoon basil (more if desired)
- Cooked shell macaroni (optional)

OPTIONAL GARNISHES

- Croutons
- Crackers
- Grated cheese
- Sour cream

Melt butter in a large saucepan. Add flour and salt; stir to form a smooth paste. Gradually add milk, stirring to blend. Cook until slightly thickened. Gradually add tomato juice. Add sugar and basil. Cook until heated through. Add macaroni, if desired. Garnish with croutons, crackers, cheese, or sour cream, if desired.

Serves 5 to 6

Family Tip: Pick one night a week to set aside for a special, once-a-week dinner. Take turns choosing the menu for dinner. The "special" person gets to choose whatever he or she wants for dinner and, with a parent's help if needed, prepare the meal.

CREAMY VEGETABLE SOUP

Serve this soup with sourdough bread or corn bread.

1	onion, chopped
3 to 4	cloves garlic, minced
1	tablespoon olive oil
1	bag (16 ounces) baby carrots
2	cups cauliflower or broccoli, chopped
2	cans (14 ounces each) chicken broth
¼	teaspoon salt, or to taste
1	teaspoon coarsely ground pepper
3	cups water
3	medium potatoes, peeled and chopped
½ to 1	cup milk or half-and-half

In a large soup pot or Dutch oven, sauté onion and garlic in olive oil until tender. Add carrots, cauliflower or broccoli, chicken broth, salt, pepper, and water. Bring to a boil. Reduce heat, cover, and simmer for 15 minutes. Add potatoes and simmer 30 minutes more, or until vegetables are tender. In a blender or food processor, blend soup in portions until smooth. Return puree to pot and add milk or half-and-half. Heat through, but do not boil.

Serves 6

CAULIFLOWER SOUP

A satisfying soup on a chilly fall evening.

1	medium head cauliflower, cut into small florets
1	small onion, chopped
⅛ to ¼	cup butter
2	tablespoons flour
2	cups chicken broth
2	cups half-and-half or milk
½	teaspoon Worcestershire sauce
½	teaspoon salt
1	cup grated cheddar cheese
	Minced chives or parsley

Put cauliflower florets in a soup pot or large saucepan. Barely cover with salted water. Cook until tender, about 8 to 10 minutes. Drain, reserving liquid, and set aside.

In the same pan, sauté onion in butter. Blend in flour, stirring until smooth. Add chicken broth, stirring until it boils. Stir in 1 cup of the cauliflower liquid, cream or milk, Worcestershire sauce, and salt (taste soup before adding salt). Add cooked cauliflower and heat through. Stir in grated cheese. Sprinkle with chives or parsley before serving.

Serves 6 to 8

Family Tip: Have a weekly family planning meeting that includes putting dinner on the schedule.

BROCCOLI CHEESE SOUP

There's almost no food more comforting than a bowl of home-made soup.

1½ pounds fresh broccoli, cut in florets or 2 packages (10 ounces each) frozen chopped broccoli
3 tablespoons butter
½ small onion, chopped
3 tablespoons flour
2 cups chicken broth
2 cups half-and-half or milk
1 teaspoon salt
¼ teaspoon nutmeg
1½ cups grated cheddar cheese

Place broccoli in a large saucepan. Barely cover with water. Cook until tender, about 8 to 10 minutes. Drain and set aside. Melt butter in a large saucepan or soup pot and sauté onion. Stir in flour and cook until thickened and smooth. Slowly add broth and half-and-half or milk. Stir and cook until thickened. Add salt, nutmeg, and cooked broccoli. Add cheese, stirring until melted.

Serves 4 to 6

BUTTERNUT SQUASH SOUP

A superb soup! Top with croutons, minced fresh parsley or cilantro, or a dollop of sour cream.

4	cups or 1 medium to large butternut squash (or other winter squash such as hubbard, acorn, pumpkin)
3 to 3½	cups apple cider or chicken broth
1½ to 2	tablespoons butter
¾	cup chopped sweet onion
2 to 3	teaspoons minced fresh ginger
2	cups half-and-half or whipping cream
	Salt to taste, about 1 to 1¼ teaspoons

SQUASH PREPARATION: METHOD 1

Peel and seed squash and cut into 1-inch cubes. Put squash in a large soup pot or saucepan. Barely cover with water. Cook until tender. Drain and puree in a food processor or blender, adding a little cider or chicken broth to thin.

SQUASH PREPARATION: METHOD 2

Cut squash in half. Remove seeds. Place cut side down on a baking sheet that is greased or sprayed with nonstick cooking spray. Bake at 400° F for about an hour, until squash can be pierced with a fork. Cool. Scoop out pulp and puree in a food processor or blender, adding a little cider or chicken broth to thin.

Melt butter in soup pot or large saucepan and sauté onion and ginger until tender. Add squash, cider or chicken broth, half-and-half or cream, and salt, stirring to mix. Put mixture in a food processor or blender in portions and blend until smooth. Return to pan. Heat soup through but do not allow to boil.

Serves 4 to 5

SPICY TOMATO SOUP

Thick and chunky with just the right amount of spice.

1 medium onion, finely chopped
1 tablespoon butter
2 cans (14½ ounces) diced tomatoes
3 cups chicken broth
1 teaspoon basil
1 teaspoon paprika
1 bay leaf
½ teaspoon ground cloves
¼ teaspoon nutmeg
½ teaspoon pepper
1 tablespoon sugar

In a large saucepan or soup pot, sauté onion in butter. Add tomatoes, chicken broth, basil, paprika, bay leaf, cloves, nutmeg, pepper, and sugar. Simmer for 20 minutes. Remove bay leaf before serving.

Serves 4

VERY EASY CHILI

Very easy and very satisfying.

½ to ¾ pound ground beef
1 large onion, chopped
2 cans (15¼ ounces each) red kidney beans, rinsed and drained
1 can (15 ounces) tomato sauce
1 can (28 ounces) diced tomatoes
1 tablespoon sugar
2 tablespoons chili powder (more, if desired)
1 to 2 teaspoons salt (to taste)

In a large saucepan or soup pot, brown ground beef with onions. Drain grease. Add kidney beans, tomato sauce, tomatoes, sugar, chili powder, and salt. If needed, add a small amount of water to thin. Bring to a boil, reduce heat, and simmer, covered, for 2 to 3 hours.

Serves 6

SOUTHWEST CHILI

This chili can also be made in a slow cooker. Brown ground beef before adding other ingredients. Cook on low heat 6 to 8 hours or high heat 3 to 4 hours.

½ pound ground beef
1 green pepper, diced
½ cup chopped onion
3 cups water
1 can (15 ounces) pinto beans, with liquid
1 can (15¼ ounces) kidney beans, with liquid
1 can (10 ounces) tomatoes and green chiles, with liquid
1 teaspoon chili powder (more, if desired)
½ teaspoon cumin
1 teaspoon salt
¼ teaspoon pepper
   Flour tortillas
   Grated Monterey Jack cheese

In a large soup pot, brown ground beef. Remove from pan and drain all but a small amount of grease. Sauté green pepper and onion in grease until soft. Return ground beef to pot and add water, pinto beans, kidney beans, and tomatoes and chiles. Stir in chili powder, cumin, salt, and pepper.

Bring soup to a boil, reduce heat, and simmer for 20 to 30 minutes. While soup is cooking, warm tortillas in oven or microwave.

Ladle soup into bowls and sprinkle with cheese. Serve with tortillas for dipping.

Serves 6 to 8

WHITE CHILI

This unusual chili will become very popular with your family.

3	cans (15½ ounces) Great Northern beans, with liquid
3+	cups chicken broth
1 to 2	cloves garlic, minced
2	medium onions, chopped and divided
1	tablespoon oil
2	cans (4 ounces each) diced green chiles (or to taste)
2	teaspoons cumin
1½	teaspoons oregano
¼	teaspoon cloves
¼	teaspoon cayenne pepper
4	cups cooked, diced chicken breasts
2 to 3	cups grated Monterey Jack cheese

OPTIONAL GARNISHES

Chopped green onions
Chopped parsley
Chopped tomatoes
Guacamole
Crushed corn chips
Salsa
Sliced olives
Sour cream

Put beans in a large soup pot or Dutch oven with broth, garlic, and half of the onions. Bring to a boil; reduce heat and simmer 30 minutes. In another pan, sauté remaining onions in oil. Add to beans. Add chiles, cumin, oregano, cloves, cayenne pepper, and chicken. Simmer 1 hour.

Ladle into bowls. Sprinkle with cheese and serve with choice of garnishes.

Serves 10 to 12

TORTELLINI SOUP WITH SAUSAGE

Serve soup in edible bread bowls, which can be purchased at most grocery store bakeries.

½ to 1 pound bulk Italian sausage (mild)
2 to 3 zucchini, sliced
1 onion, chopped
2 cups sliced mushrooms
1 clove garlic, minced
1 teaspoon oregano
6 cups chicken broth
1 can (28 ounces) diced tomatoes
1 can (6 ounces) tomato paste
1 can (8 ounces) tomato sauce
1 package (9 ounces) fresh tortellini
  Grated fresh Parmesan cheese

In a large soup pot or Dutch oven, sauté sausage until it is cooked and crumbly. Drain grease. Sauté zucchini, onion, mushrooms, and garlic in pot with sausage. Add oregano, chicken broth, tomatoes, tomato paste, and tomato sauce. Stir to blend. Bring to a boil. Add tortellini. Reduce heat and simmer for 10 to 15 minutes, until tortellini is cooked al dente. Serve with Parmesan cheese.

Serves 8 to 10

MEXICAN MINESTRONE

Bring your family to the table with this unusual minestrone soup.

1 cup chopped onion
1 teaspoon olive oil
½ teaspoon oregano
½ teaspoon cumin
2 cloves garlic, minced
6 cups chicken broth
2 cups diced potatoes, cooked
1 can (15 ounces) garbanzo beans
2 cups cooked, diced chicken
Salt and pepper to taste
1 cup frozen corn, thawed
1 cup diced zucchini
1 cup diced fresh tomatoes or canned diced tomatoes
½ cup minced cilantro

GARNISHES

Grated Monterey Jack cheese
Sour cream
Lime wedges

In a large saucepan or soup pot, sauté onion in olive oil until tender, about 3 minutes. Add oregano, cumin, and garlic, and sauté for 1 minute. Add chicken broth, cooked potatoes, garbanzo beans, and chicken. Add salt and pepper to taste. Cook for 5 minutes. Add corn and zucchini; cook for 5 minutes more. Add tomatoes and ⅓ cup cilantro. Cook for 3 minutes and remove from heat. Do not overcook or soup will lose its fresh taste. Serve with remaining cilantro, cheese, sour cream, and lime wedges.

Serves 6 to 8

Family Tip: If a member of your family is living away from home, arrange to have dinnertime conference calls on occasion. This will allow everyone in the family to talk to the absent family member, making it seem for a moment as if he or she is at home for dinner.

FRENCH ONION SOUP

A classic worth repeating often.

2	slices bacon, cut in 1-inch pieces
2 to 3	large onions, thinly sliced or chopped
2	cloves garlic, minced
1	tablespoon tarragon vinegar
1	tablespoon red wine vinegar
½	teaspoon Tabasco sauce
2	teaspoons Worcestershire sauce
1	teaspoon thyme
2	tablespoons dried parsley or ¼ cup minced fresh parsley
	Freshly ground pepper to taste
6	cups chicken broth
4	slices French or other crusty bread slices, toasted
4	slices mozzarella or Monterey Jack cheese

In a large saucepan or soup pot, sauté bacon until limp. Remove bacon. Sauté onions and garlic in bacon grease about 5 minutes. Return bacon to pan. Add tarragon and red wine vinegars, Tabasco sauce, Worcestershire sauce, thyme, parsley, pepper, and chicken broth. Simmer for 20 to 30 minutes.

Toast slices of bread and place in bottom of each bowl. Put a slice of cheese on top of toast. Pour soup over top.

Serves 4

Salads

SPINACH MUSHROOM SALAD

It's still a good idea to rinse spinach even if the bag says "prewashed."

FOR SALAD:

1   bag (10 ounces) baby spinach
½   small red onion, sliced into rings
1   cup sliced mushrooms
3   hardboiled eggs, sliced
4   slices bacon, cooked and crumbled

FOR MUSTARD DRESSING:

½   small onion
¾   cup olive oil
⅓   cup cider vinegar
⅓   cup sugar
2   teaspoons prepared mustard
1   teaspoon celery seeds
½   teaspoon salt

In a salad bowl, combine spinach, onion, mushrooms, eggs, and bacon. Just before serving, toss with Mustard Dressing or Creamy Poppy Seed Dressing.

To make Mustard Dressing, in a blender or food processor, combine onion, olive oil, vinegar, sugar, mustard, celery seeds, and salt. Blend until well mixed.

You can also serve Creamy Poppy Seed Dressing with this salad (see page 67).

Serves 6

SPINACH SALAD

Baby spinach works best for spinach salads because of its size, ease of use, and appearance.

FOR SALAD:

3	cups baby spinach
3 to 4	cups or 1 head lettuce, any variety, torn
½	cup slivered almonds
1	cup grated mozzarella cheese
1 to 2	Granny Smith apples, diced
4	slices bacon, cooked and crumbled

FOR DRESSING:

½	cup sugar
1	teaspoon salt
1	teaspoon prepared mustard
¼	cup cider vinegar
⅔	cup olive oil
1	tablespoon poppy seeds
½	small onion, finely chopped

In a salad bowl, combine baby spinach, lettuce, almonds, cheese, apples, and bacon. Pour desired amount of dressing over salad just before serving.

To make dressing, in a pint jar, combine sugar, salt, mustard, vinegar, olive oil, poppy seeds, and onion. Put lid tightly on jar and shake to blend well.

Serves 6

Family Tip: Expand your family's food horizons by holding comparative tasting events. For example, buy several varieties of apples or peaches and have family members taste and compare.

STRAWBERRY SPINACH SALAD

The cheery red strawberry dressing makes this salad appealing.

FOR SALAD:

1	head red leaf lettuce, torn
3 to 4	cups or 1 bag (10 ounces) spinach
1	cup sliced strawberries
1	cup cashew halves
½ to ¾	red onion, diced
½	cup cooked and crumbled bacon pieces (optional)

FOR DRESSING:

2	tablespoons red wine vinegar
2	tablespoons sugar
½	cup olive oil
½	teaspoon dry mustard
½	teaspoon salt
½	cup strawberry jam

In a large salad bowl, combine lettuce, spinach, strawberries, cashews, onion, and bacon, if desired. Add dressing just before serving.

To make dressing, combine vinegar, sugar, olive oil, mustard, salt, and jam in a bowl or jar, mixing well until sugar dissolves.

Serves 6 to 8

Save Money: Buy fruits and vegetables in season at a produce market, where prices are generally lower than in stores.

GREEN SALAD WITH APPLES AND PEARS

The creamy citrus dressing adds a lovely flavor to this salad.

FOR SALAD:

2 tablespoons butter
2 tablespoons honey
½ cup sliced almonds
6 cups salad greens (spinach, spring mix, red or green leaf lettuce, or iceberg lettuce)
1 large apple, peeled (if desired) and diced
1 red pear, diced (with peel on)
½ cup dried cranberries or dried cherries
1 small avocado, diced
2 to 3 tablespoons diced red onion

FOR DRESSING:

2 tablespoons olive oil
2 tablespoons red wine vinegar
2 tablespoons orange juice or frozen lemonade concentrate
½ teaspoon salt
⅓ cup mayonnaise

Heat oven to 400° F. In a small pan, melt together butter and honey. Put almonds in a baking pan; pour honey mixture over and bake for 10 minutes. Stir often and watch carefully so almonds do not burn. Remove almonds from pan and put on wax paper to cool. Break into pieces.

In a large salad bowl, combine salad greens, apple, pear, dried cranberries or dried cherries, avocado, and onion. Before serving, pour desired amount of dressing on salad. Top with almonds.

To make the dressing, in a small jar, whisk together oil, vinegar, orange juice or lemonade concentrate, salt, and mayonnaise.

Serves 6

GREEN SALAD WITH CREAMY RASPBERRY DRESSING

Sure to be a winner at your table.

FOR SALAD:

1 to 2	cups romaine or iceberg lettuce, torn
1	cup green leaf lettuce, torn
1	cup red leaf lettuce, torn
1	cup diced artichoke hearts
½	cup chopped walnuts or pecans
½	cup gorgonzola or feta cheese, crumbled (optional)
½	cup whole raspberries (optional)

FOR DRESSING:

⅓	cup olive oil
3	tablespoons sugar
2	tablespoons raspberry vinegar
1	tablespoon sour cream
1½	teaspoons Dijon mustard
½	cup fresh or frozen raspberries (without syrup)

Combine lettuces in a medium salad bowl. Add artichoke hearts and walnuts or pecans. Sprinkle with gorgonzola or feta cheese, if desired. Garnish with whole raspberries, if desired. Before serving, toss with dressing.

To make dressing, in a small bowl or jar, mix olive oil, sugar, vinegar, sour cream, and mustard. Stir well to blend. Add raspberries. Refrigerate at least 1 hour to blend flavors.

Serves 4

Save Time: When you bring your groceries home from the store, immediately separate and wash all lettuce leaves. Drain lettuce in a salad spinner or colander placed in the kitchen sink. When lettuce is thoroughly drained, store it, along with a paper towel to absorb moisture, in a resealable plastic bag in the refrigerator. Lettuce will then be crisp and ready to use in salads.

SALAD DE MAISON

Using block Parmesan cheese is well worth the extra cost and the short time it takes to grate. It just tastes so much better.

FOR SALAD:

2	heads romaine lettuce, torn in small pieces
2	cups grape tomatoes or halved cherry tomatoes
1	cup grated Swiss cheese
⅔	cup slivered almonds
¼	pound bacon, cooked and diced
⅓	cup grated Parmesan cheese
	Salt and pepper to taste
	Croutons for garnish

FOR DRESSING:

	Juice of 1 lemon
2	cloves garlic, minced
1	teaspoon salt
½	teaspoon pepper
¾	cup olive oil

In a salad bowl, combine lettuce, tomatoes, Swiss cheese, almonds, and bacon. Toss with dressing, Parmesan cheese, salt, and pepper. Garnish with croutons.

To make dressing, combine lemon juice, garlic, salt, and pepper. Beating continuously with a fork, slowly add oil in a stream.

Serves 8 to 10

GREENS AND FRUIT WITH CITRUS DRESSING

A flavorful mixture of textures, colors, and tastes.

FOR SALAD:

1	bag (10 ounces) spring mix
6 to 8	cups mixed greens, such as romaine, iceberg lettuce, red or green leaf lettuce, baby spinach, or spring mix
1 to 2	oranges, peeled and segmented
1	small cucumber, sliced
1	small avocado, diced
1	apple (Fuji, Gala, or Granny Smith), diced
1	cup sliced strawberries
½	cup halved red grapes

FOR DRESSING:

½	cup frozen orange juice concentrate, thawed (measure when thawed)
½	teaspoon grated orange rind
⅓	cup olive oil
2	tablespoons sugar
2	tablespoons cider vinegar
3	teaspoons lemon juice
½	teaspoon salt

In a large salad bowl, combine spring mix and other greens, oranges, cucumber, avocado, apple, strawberries, and grapes. Add desired amount of dressing just before serving.

To make dressing, mix orange juice concentrate, orange rind, olive oil, sugar, vinegar, lemon juice, and salt in a blender or put in a jar and shake thoroughly.

Serves 6 to 8

BLEU CHEESE AND PEAR SALAD

The tanginess of bleu or feta cheese contrasts with the sweetness of the fruit in this favorite recipe.

FOR SALAD:

2	packages (5 ounces each) spring greens
½	cup crumbled bleu cheese or feta cheese
½	cup walnuts or pecans, chopped and toasted
1	cup diced pears, peeled
1	cup sliced strawberries, blueberries, and/or raspberries (optional)

FOR DRESSING:

⅓	cup raspberry vinegar
1	teaspoon salt
⅓	cup sugar
1	tablespoon dry mustard
1½	tablespoons minced onion
1	cup olive oil
1	tablespoon poppy seeds

In a large serving bowl, combine greens, cheese, nuts, and pears. Add strawberries, blueberries, and/or raspberries, if desired. Before serving, pour dressing over greens and toss to coat.

To make dressing, combine vinegar, salt, sugar, dry mustard, onion, olive oil, and poppy seeds; mix well.

Serves 8

Cooking Tip: Use a melon baller to core a pear. Slice the pear in half lengthwise. Remove the core with the melon baller, then draw the melon baller to the top of the pear to remove the interior stem.

ORANGE AVOCADO SALAD WITH CITRUS VINAIGRETTE

Avocados taste best when fully ripe. To help them ripen more quickly, place them in a paper bag and set them on the counter for a day or two.

FOR SALAD:

5 to 6	cups variety of salad greens, torn
2	oranges, segmented
½	grapefruit, segmented
2	avocados, diced
½	cup dried cranberries or dried cherries
⅓ to ½	cup pine nuts or pistachio nuts
	Feta or gorgonzola cheese (for garnish)

FOR DRESSING:

1	lime
1	orange
½	grapefruit
½	lemon
	1 tablespoon Dijon mustard
	1 teaspoon sugar
	Salt and pepper to taste
½	cup olive oil

In a salad bowl, combine salad greens, oranges and grapefruit sections, avocados, dried cranberries or dried cherries, and pine nuts or pistachio nuts. Before serving, add desired amount of dressing. Sprinkle with feta or gorgonzola cheese.

To make dressing, juice lime, orange, grapefruit, and lemon. Whisk juices with mustard, sugar, salt, and pepper. Add oil; stir vigorously or put in a jar and shake. Adjust seasonings to taste.

Serves 6

Substitute grapefruit for the oranges or use a combination of both.

3   oranges, peeled and diced
2   tomatoes, diced
2   avocados, diced
½   cup diced red onion
3   tablespoons minced cilantro
⅓   cup olive oil
¼   cup fresh lime juice
      Salt and freshly ground pepper

In a glass salad bowl, combine oranges, tomatoes, avocados, onion, and cilantro.

Whisk olive oil and lime juice until blended. Add salt and pepper to taste. Pour on salad, stirring gently to coat. Chill ½ hour before serving.

Serves 4

Family Tip: Eat together around a table so that family members can see and converse with each other.

CARROT RAISIN SALAD

Sour cream and coconut perk up this old favorite.

- 3 cups grated or julienned carrots
- 1 cup raisins
- ½ cup flaked coconut
- ¼ cup diced red or sweet onion
- 1 cup sour cream
- ½ teaspoon salt

In a medium salad bowl, mix carrots, raisins, coconut, onion, sour cream, and salt. Chill before serving.

Serves 4 to 6

LEMON PIE SALAD

Rich and creamy, this salad goes well with plain meats, such as ham, steak, or roast beef.

- 1 package (3 ounces) lemon pie filling (not instant)
- ½ pint heavy cream, whipped or 2 cups Cool Whip
- 1 can (20 ounces) pineapple tidbits, drained
- 1 can (11 ounces) mandarin oranges
- 2 bananas, sliced
- 1 cup miniature marshmallows (optional)

In a medium saucepan, cook pie filling as directed on package. Cool. Fold whipped cream into pie filling in a large bowl. Add pineapple, mandarin oranges, bananas, and marshmallows, if using. Chill well before serving.

Serves 8 to 10

Save Time: A food processor can save considerable time. Use it to chop onions; slice or shred carrots, cabbage, celery, green peppers, or cheese; or to make bread crumbs.

41

CHRISTMAS SALAD

This salad offers the colors of Christmas in a festive arrangement.

FOR DRESSING:

¼ cup olive oil
¼ cup fresh lemon juice
½ teaspoon salt
¼ teaspoon freshly ground black pepper
1 tablespoon honey

FOR SALAD:

1 can (15 ounces) cannellini (white kidney) beans
1 large green pepper, cut into bite-size pieces
1 cucumber, cut into bite-size pieces
½ head red cabbage, coarsely chopped
1 bunch radishes, quartered
1 cup grape tomatoes or halved cherry tomatoes
1 cup feta or bleu cheese, crumbled
2 tablespoons minced Italian parsley

In a small lidded jar, mix olive oil, lemon juice, salt, pepper, and honey.

To make salad, two to four hours ahead of serving, place beans, green pepper, cucumber, cabbage, radishes, and tomatoes into separate resealable plastic bags. Add 1 to 2 tablespoons of dressing to each bag.* Chill, turning bags several times to distribute dressing.

To serve, arrange rows of beans, green pepper, cucumber, cabbage, radishes, tomatoes, and feta or bleu cheese on a large platter. Sprinkle with chopped parsley.

*Dressing may be doubled for a moister salad.

Serves 8 to 10

LAYERED VEGETABLE SALAD

Use any combination of vegetables you wish.

FOR SALAD:

3 to 4	cups romaine, iceberg, or red leaf lettuce, torn in bite-size pieces
¾ to 1	cup beets, julienned or diced
¾ to 1	cup cucumber, sliced
¾ to 1	cup red pepper, thinly sliced
¾ to 1	cup mushrooms, sliced
¾ to 1	cup carrots, sliced
¾ to 1	cup fresh green beans or broccoli, cooked crisp-tender and cooled
¾ to 1	cup tomatoes, diced
¾ to 1	cup avocado, diced
¾ to 1	cup green onions, chopped (or red onion, thinly sliced)
¾ to 1	cup frozen peas, thawed
¾ to 1	cup frozen corn, thawed
½	cup croutons for garnish

FOR BALSAMIC VINAIGRETTE:

¼	cup olive oil
¼	cup balsamic vinegar
¼	teaspoon salt
	Pepper to taste
2	teaspoons sugar

Place lettuce in a large glass salad bowl. Use as many or few of the different vegetables as you prefer. Layer the vegetables. Do not mix the salad. Pour desired amount of dressing over the top.

To make Balsamic Vinaigrette, whisk together oil, vinegar, salt, pepper, and sugar in a small bowl or put in a jar with a lid and shake.

Serves 8 to 10

COLESLAW

Coleslaw is a tradition with barbecued ribs, but you'll want to serve this with many different meals.

- ½ head shredded green cabbage (about 2 cups)
- ½ head shredded red cabbage (about 1 cup)
- 1 cup grated carrots
- 2 cans (8 ounces each) crushed pineapple, drained
- ¾ cup mayonnaise or Ranch dressing

In a medium salad bowl, mix green cabbage, red cabbage, and carrots. In a small bowl, mix pineapple with mayonnaise or Ranch dressing. Pour over salad and mix well. Chill before serving.

Serves 6 to 8

BROCCOLI SLAW

An unusual coleslaw. You can vary the amounts of salad ingredients that appeal to you.

- 1 bag (16 ounces) broccoli slaw (available in produce section)
- 1 can (11 ounces) mandarin oranges
- 1 cup red grapes, halved
- 1 cup strawberries, sliced
- ½ to ¾ cup dried cranberries
- 2 to 3 tablespoons chopped red onion
  Creamy Poppy Seed Dressing (see page 67)

In a salad bowl, combine broccoli slaw, mandarin oranges, grapes, strawberries, dried cranberries, and onion. Stir in desired amount of dressing.

Serves 6 to 8

ORIENTAL SALAD

This salad has a distinctive and excellent dressing that goes well on other green salads too.

FOR SALAD:

1	head iceberg lettuce, torn in small pieces
2	medium carrots, grated
1	cup dried cranberries
⅓	cup sliced almonds
¼	cup sunflower seeds
1	medium cucumber, chopped
1	large tomato, diced
1	cup coarsely chopped sugar or snow peas
	Croutons

FOR DRESSING:

¼	cup cider vinegar
¼	cup soy sauce
2	tablespoons sesame oil
½ to 1	teaspoon hot chili oil
½	teaspoon salt
2	teaspoons sugar
1	clove garlic, minced
1 to 2	teaspoons finely grated ginger or 1 tablespoon bottled minced ginger

In a large salad bowl, mix lettuce, carrots, cranberries, almonds, sunflower seeds, cucumber, tomato, and sugar or snow peas. Add amount of dressing desired to salad and toss lightly. Top with croutons. Serve immediately.

To make dressing, whisk together vinegar, soy sauce, sesame oil, chili oil, salt, sugar, garlic, and ginger in a small, deep bowl or pint jar.

Serves 6 to 8

UPDATED WALDORF SALAD

Waldorf Salad originated at the Waldorf Astoria Hotel in New York City. New ingredients update an old favorite.

3	large apples, unpeeled and chopped
3	tablespoons + 1 teaspoon fresh orange juice, divided
1	teaspoon grated orange peel
⅔	cup chopped celery
½	cup dried cranberries or dried cherries
½	cup mayonnaise
¼	teaspoon ground cloves
1	tablespoon sugar
½	cup whipping cream, whipped
½	cup chopped walnuts or pecans

In a medium bowl, toss apples with 3 tablespoons orange juice, orange peel, celery, and dried cranberries or dried cherries.

In a small bowl, mix mayonnaise, cloves, 1 teaspoon orange juice, sugar, and whipped cream. Stir into fruit. Cover bowl and chill for 1 to 2 hours. Add nuts just before serving.

Serves 6 to 8

Cooking Tip: Freeze nuts, both shelled and unshelled, to keep them longer. It is easier to crack shelled nuts when they are frozen.

MANDARIN YOGURT SALAD

You won't find this tasty dressing in a bottle on the store shelf.

FOR SALAD:

- ½   cup sliced almonds
- 2   tablespoons sugar
- ½   head iceberg lettuce
- 1   head red leaf or romaine lettuce, or equivalent amount of spinach
- 1   cup chopped celery
- 2   green onions, chopped
- 1   can (11 ounces) mandarin oranges, drained

FOR DRESSING:

- 1   can (11 ounces) mandarin oranges, drained
- 1   carton (6 ounces) orange yogurt
- ⅓   cup mayonnaise

In a small skillet, cook almonds and sugar, stirring constantly, until almonds are coated and sugar is dissolved. Be careful not to burn. Cool.

In a salad bowl, combine lettuces, celery, green onions, and mandarin oranges. Toss salad with dressing. Sprinkle with almonds and serve.

To make dressing, in a small bowl, mash mandarin oranges with a fork. Stir in yogurt and mayonnaise.

Serves 6

RASPBERRY TAPIOCA SALAD

*Refreshing! Try various combinations, such as strawberry Jell-O
and frozen strawberries or orange Jell-O and mandarin oranges.*

    3   cups water
    1   package (3 ounces) raspberry Jell-O
    1   package (3.4 ounces) instant vanilla pudding
    1   package (3 ounces) tapioca pudding
    1   package (10 ounces) frozen raspberries, thawed
    1   can (8 ounces) crushed pineapple, drained
    1   carton (8 ounces) Cool Whip, thawed

In a large saucepan, bring water to a boil. Stir in Jell-O, vanilla pudding, and tapioca pudding with a whisk. Bring to a boil again, stirring constantly. Boil for 1 minute. Remove from heat and cool. Fold in raspberries, pineapple, and Cool Whip. Chill in refrigerator 2 hours or more.

Serves 12

FROZEN CRANBERRY SALAD

This salad may become a new tradition in your home.

    2   packages (3 ounces) cream cheese, softened
    2   tablespoons sugar
    2   tablespoons mayonnaise or Miracle Whip
    1   can (16 ounces) whole-berry cranberry sauce
    1   can (8 ounces) crushed pineapple, drained
    ½   cup chopped walnuts or pecans
    1   cup whipping cream, whipped
 3 to 4 drops red food coloring

In a large bowl, beat cream cheese with sugar and mayonnaise or Miracle Whip until well mixed. Stir in cranberry sauce, pineapple, and nuts. Fold in whipped cream and food coloring. Put into a loaf pan and freeze until firm. Soften at room temperature for 10 to 15 minutes before serving. Unmold; slice to serve.

Serves 8 to 10

COOKIE FRUIT SALAD

Children will enjoy helping prepare this salad. How many salads include cookies?

- 1 package (5¼ ounces) instant vanilla pudding
- 1½ cups milk
- 1 carton (8 ounces) Cool Whip or ½ to ¾ cup whipping cream, whipped
- 2 cans (11 ounces each) mandarin oranges, drained
- 1 can (20 ounces) pineapple chunks, drained
- 1 package (11½ ounces) chocolate striped shortbread cookies, chopped
- 2 bananas, sliced

Mix pudding and milk together with a wire whisk. Add Cool Whip or whipped cream and mix well. Fold in mandarin oranges, pineapple chunks, cookies, and bananas. Chill before serving.

Serves 12

Family Tip: If eating dinner together is happening infrequently, hold a family meeting to evaluate the kinds and number of outside activities that are occupying family members at dinnertime. Enlist family members' support to improve the situation.

BERRY GOOD FRUIT SALAD

The array of fruit colors in this salad is "berry" attractive in a glass bowl.

1	banana, sliced
2	nectarines or peaches, diced and peeled
2	kiwifruits, sliced and peeled
1	pint blueberries
1	pint strawberries, sliced
1½	cups watermelon balls or chunks
1	cup red or green grapes, cut in halves
½	cup lime juice
½	cup water
¼ to ⅓	cup sugar

In a large salad bowl, combine bananas, nectarines or peaches, kiwi, blueberries, strawberries, watermelon, and grapes. Mix lime juice, water, and sugar together in a small bowl. Pour over fruit. Refrigerate 1 hour before serving.

Serves 6 to 8

Save Money: Forgo as many convenience foods as you can; for example, sweetened cereals, precut and washed salad greens, frozen vegetables with sauces, precut fruits such as watermelon and cantaloupe, baking mixes, and spaghetti sauce.

FRUIT WITH MAPLE CREAM DRESSING

Excellent with most fruits, but particularly wonderful with strawberries.

¼	cup pure maple syrup
2	tablespoons brown sugar
1	cup sour cream
2	tablespoons whipping cream
4 to 6	cups fresh fruit such as:
	Apples, diced
	Bananas, sliced
	Blackberries
	Blueberries
	Cantaloupe, diced
	Honeydew melon, diced
	Kiwifruit, sliced
	Mangoes, diced
	Peaches, sliced
	Pineapple, diced
	Red or green grapes, halved
	Raspberries
	Strawberries, sliced

Put maple syrup, brown sugar, and sour cream in a deep bowl. Using an electric mixer, beat on low until well mixed. Add whipping cream and beat on high for 2 minutes. Pour over a bowl of fresh fruit.

Makes about 1½ cups dressing

FRUIT WITH CINNAMON-HONEY DRESSING

The lemon juice keeps the fruit from darkening; the honey and cinnamon add sweetness and spice.

½ cup fresh lemon juice
2 tablespoons honey
½ teaspoon cinnamon (or more to taste)
4 to 6 cups fresh fruit, such as:
  Apples, diced
  Bananas, sliced
  Blackberries
  Blueberries
  Cantaloupe, diced
  Honeydew melon, diced
  Kiwifruit, sliced
  Mangoes, diced
  Peaches, diced
  Pineapple, diced
  Red or green grapes, halved
  Raspberries
  Strawberries, sliced

Put lemon juice, honey, and cinnamon in a small bowl; mix well. Pour over a combination of fresh fruits.

Chill before serving.

Makes ½ cup dressing

SWEET POTATO SALAD

Who says potato salad has to be made with white potatoes?

4 to 5	sweet potatoes or yams
1	cup sliced celery
2	tablespoons sliced green onions
2	tablespoons sweet pickle relish
1	teaspoon salt
¼	cup mayonnaise
¼	cup sour cream
½ to ¾	cup pecan halves, toasted

Cook sweet potatoes or yams in a large pan of water until tender, about 25 to 30 minutes. Drain and cool. Peel sweet potatoes or yams and cut into 1-inch cubes.

In a medium bowl, combine celery, green onions, relish, salt, mayonnaise, and sour cream. Toss with yams or sweet potatoes to coat. Cover and chill at least 2 hours or overnight. Add pecans just before serving.

Serves 6 to 8

Save Time: Toast nuts, such as almonds and pecans, in the microwave. Place nuts in a glass bowl and microwave, uncovered, on high for 2 minutes. Stir and microwave 1 more minute.

RED POTATO SALAD

Red potatoes provide an interesting change from the usual potato salad.

8 to 10 medium red potatoes
1½ tablespoons sweet pickle relish
1 teaspoon prepared mustard
2 teaspoons sugar
½ cup Miracle Whip
1 tablespoon mayonnaise
½ teaspoon salt
⅛ teaspoon pepper
1 tablespoon finely chopped onion
4 eggs, hardboiled and chopped
½ cup whipping cream, whipped

In a large saucepan, boil potatoes in their skins about 30 minutes. Cool in cold water. Cube. Combine pickle relish, mustard, sugar, Miracle Whip, mayonnaise, salt, pepper, onion, eggs, and whipped cream. Add potatoes, stirring gently to combine. Season to taste.

Serves 6 to 8

CHICKEN SALAD WITH STRAWBERRY DRESSING

You can also make this without the chicken for a festive dinner salad.

FOR SALAD:

3 to 4	boneless, skinless chicken breasts
1	can (14½ ounces) chicken broth
6	cups mixed salad greens, torn
3 to 4	green onions, sliced
2	cups sliced fresh strawberries
1	avocado, diced
½	cup chopped pecans

FOR STRAWBERRY DRESSING:

½	cup strawberries
⅓	cup orange juice
2	tablespoons olive oil
1	tablespoon fresh lemon juice
	Grated peel of 1 small lemon
1	teaspoon sugar
½	teaspoon chili powder
¼	teaspoon salt
¼	teaspoon pepper

In a medium saucepan, cook chicken in broth about 20 minutes (add a little water if needed.) Drain. When cool, cut in bite-size pieces. Mix with salad greens, onions, strawberries, avocado, and pecans. Toss with Strawberry Dressing.

To make Strawberry Dressing, put strawberries, orange juice, olive oil, lemon juice, lemon peel, sugar, chili powder, salt, and pepper in a blender or food processor. Blend until smooth.

Serves 4 to 6

CHICKEN RICE SALAD

Rice makes appearances in many dishes, whether it's a side dish, main dish, dessert, or salad—as here.

FOR SALAD:

2½ cups cooked, diced chicken — see p. 55
 2 cups cooked rice, chilled
 1 cup halved seedless red grapes
 1 cup chopped celery
 1 can (11 ounces) mandarin oranges
 1 can (20 ounces) pineapple chunks or tidbits
¾ cup sliced almonds

FOR DRESSING:

1 tablespoon olive oil
1 tablespoon orange juice
1 tablespoon red wine vinegar
½ teaspoon salt (or more to taste)
¾ cup mayonnaise

In a large bowl, combine chicken, rice, grapes, celery, mandarin oranges, pineapple, and almonds. Combine dressing with chicken mixture. Chill before serving.

To make dressing, in a small bowl, mix olive oil, orange juice, vinegar, salt, and mayonnaise.

Serves 4 to 6

Family Tip: If your older children live throughout the world or are away at college, share recipes via phone, e-mail, or a family website.

TROPICAL CHICKEN SALAD

Serve this when you're longing for a taste of the tropics.

2   cups cooked, cubed chicken — *see 55*
1   cup chopped celery
1   cup mayonnaise
½ to 1   teaspoon curry powder
1   can (20 ounces) pineapple chunks, drained
2   bananas, sliced
1   can (11 ounces) mandarin oranges
½   cup flaked coconut
     Salad greens
¾   cup salted peanuts, cashew halves, or chopped pecans

Place chicken and celery in a large bowl. In a small bowl, combine mayonnaise and curry; add to chicken and mix well. Cover and chill 30 minutes.

Just before serving, add pineapple, bananas, mandarin oranges, and coconut; toss gently. Serve on a bed of salad greens. Sprinkle with nuts.

Serves 6

CHICKEN, DILL, AND PASTA SALAD

This salad is perfect for a summer evening supper. Serve with fresh fruit and nice bread.

- ¾ cup mayonnaise
- ¾ cup sour cream
- 1 tablespoon dried dill weed
- 1 tablespoon onion salt
- 2 cups cooked and cubed chicken, cooled — See p. 55
- 2 cups halved red grapes
- 2 cups chopped celery
- 1 package (12 ounces) large shell macaroni, cooked, drained, and cooled

In a small bowl, mix mayonnaise, sour cream, dill weed, and onion salt.

In a glass salad bowl, combine chicken, grapes, celery, and macaroni. Stir in mayonnaise mixture. Chill before serving.

Serves 8 to 10

GRILLED CHICKEN SALAD

Ingredients can be varied according to taste. Try it without chicken for a great green salad.

2   boneless, skinless chicken breasts
     Salt and pepper or lemon pepper
1   head romaine lettuce, torn
2   Granny Smith apples, unpeeled and diced
1   cup walnut halves
1   cup dried cranberries or dried cherries
½   cup bleu or feta cheese, crumbled
     Newman's Own Balsamic Vinaigrette

Season chicken with salt and pepper or lemon pepper and grill or broil until cooked through. Cool; cut into bite-size pieces.

Put lettuce, apples, walnuts, and dried cranberries or cherries in a salad bowl. Add diced chicken and bleu or feta cheese and gently mix. Just prior to serving add enough vinaigrette to lightly moisten salad.

Serves 4 to 6

Save Time: Quickly dry salad greens with a salad spinner.

PECAN-RIMMED CHICKEN SALAD

A little more work, but sure to get five-star reviews.

FOR SALAD:

3	boneless, skinless chicken breasts, cut in halves
2	egg whites
2	teaspoons cornstarch
	Juice of ½ lemon
1 ¼	cups coarse dry bread crumbs
1	teaspoon salt
¼	teaspoon pepper
1	tablespoon minced fresh parsley
¾	cup chopped pecans
¾	teaspoon oregano
¾	teaspoon thyme
½	teaspoon paprika
¼	teaspoon cayenne pepper
2	tablespoons olive oil or butter
6 to 8	cups salad greens (spring mix, spinach, romaine, or red leaf)
½	cup feta, gorgonzola, or bleu cheese
½	small red onion, sliced

FOR HONEY MUSTARD DRESSING:

¼	cup honey
2 to 3	tablespoons Dijon or spicy brown mustard
3	tablespoons olive oil
1	tablespoon chopped green onions or shallot
1	tablespoon cider vinegar
	Juice of ½ lemon
1	teaspoon grated lemon peel
	Salt and pepper to taste

Place chicken breasts and a tablespoon of water inside a resealable plastic bag. Using a meat pounder or mallet, pound chicken breasts to about ½ inch thick.

In a shallow bowl, blend egg whites, cornstarch, and lemon juice. In another shallow bowl, combine bread crumbs, salt, pepper, parsley, pecans, oregano, thyme, paprika, and cayenne pepper. Dip chicken pieces first in egg white mixture, then in bread crumb mixture. Heat oven to 450° F. Heat oil or butter in a large skillet (ovenproof if available) and sauté chicken on both sides until light brown and crisp. Put chicken in a baking dish or keep in ovenproof skillet and bake 8 to 10 minutes. When cool, cut into bite-size pieces.

In a large salad bowl, combine salad greens, cheese, onion, and chicken. Pour desired amount of Honey Mustard Dressing over salad just before serving.

To make Honey Mustard Dressing, combine honey, mustard, olive oil, green onions or shallot, vinegar, lemon juice, and lemon peel. Whisk until well blended. Add salt and pepper to taste.

Serves 6

OLD-FASHIONED MACARONI SALAD

Reminiscent of the past—perhaps your grandmother made this salad.

- 8 ounces shell macaroni, cooked according to package directions, drained, and cooled
- 1 cup grated cheddar cheese
- 1 cup diced ham
- 1 can (2¼ ounces) sliced olives
- 4 hard boiled eggs, diced or sliced
- 1 small bunch green onions, sliced
- ¾ cup mayonnaise
  Garlic salt to taste
  Onion powder to taste

In a large salad bowl, mix macaroni, cheese, ham, olives, eggs, and green onions. Add mayonnaise and stir to combine. Add garlic salt and onion powder to taste. Chill before serving.

Serves 6 to 8

SOUTHWEST STEAK SALAD

Fix a different main-dish salad often during the warm summer months.

FOR SALAD:

3	tablespoons olive oil
2	tablespoons lime juice
2	tablespoons soy sauce
1	tablespoon water
1 ¼	teaspoons lemon pepper
1	teaspoon garlic powder
½ to 1	pound sirloin steak, cut in ½-inch strips
6	cups assorted salad greens
1	small red pepper, cut in strips
1	small yellow pepper, cut in strips
2 to 3	green onions, sliced
	Guacamole
	Sour cream (optional)
2 to 3	tablespoons chopped cilantro
	Tortilla chips

FOR GUACAMOLE:

2	large ripe avocados, mashed
1	large tomato, diced
¼	medium onion, finely diced
1	clove garlic, minced
1	teaspoon fresh lime or lemon juice
1	can (4 ounces) diced green chiles (to taste)
	Salt to taste

Combine olive oil, lime juice, soy sauce, water, lemon pepper, and garlic powder in a shallow glass baking dish or a resealable plastic bag. Add steak strips, turning to coat evenly. Marinate for ½ hour.

Arrange salad greens on individual serving plates or in a large bowl. Set aside.

Put steak strips in a large skillet. Cook over high heat, 3 or 4 minutes, stirring constantly. Arrange steak strips over salad greens. Top with red and yellow peppers and green onions. Add a dollop of guacamole and sour cream, if desired. Sprinkle with cilantro. Serve with tortilla chips.

To make Guacamole, in a medium bowl, combine avocados, tomato, onion, garlic, lime or lemon juice, green chiles, and salt. Chill 1 to 2 hours before serving for optimum taste.

Serves 4 to 6

TORTELLINI SALAD

Be creative! Add a variety of fresh vegetables to this versatile salad.

12	ounces cheese-filled tortellini, cooked according to package directions and drained
½	can (14½ ounces) hearts of palm, sliced into ½-inch pieces
1	jar (6½ ounces) artichoke hearts, chopped
1	cup sliced mushrooms
3 to 4	green onions, sliced
1 to 2	cups broccoli florets
¼	cup sliced olives (more, if desired)
1	cup diced tomatoes
	Creamy Italian dressing

In a large salad bowl, combine tortellini, hearts of palm, artichoke hearts, mushrooms, green onions, broccoli, olives, and tomatoes. Add enough dressing to moisten salad and serve.

Serves 6 to 8

SANTA FE CHICKEN CAESAR SALAD

What a great main-course salad this is! Fresh fruit and rolls could round out the meal.

3	tablespoons olive oil
2	tablespoons lime juice
1	teaspoon cumin
1	clove garlic, minced
½	teaspoon chili powder
½	teaspoon salt
¼	teaspoon pepper
	Dash cayenne pepper
3 to 4	boneless, skinless chicken breasts, cubed
1 to 1½	cups frozen or canned corn
½ to 1	can (15 ounces) black or kidney beans, rinsed and drained
½	cup diced jicama
3 to 4	green onions, sliced
1	avocado, diced
1 to 2	heads romaine lettuce, torn
	Newman's Own Creamy Caesar Salad Dressing
	Grated Parmesan cheese
	Seasoned croutons (optional)

In a small bowl, combine olive oil, lime juice, cumin, garlic, chili powder, salt, pepper, and cayenne pepper. Blend well. Marinate chicken in mixture in a resealable plastic bag or covered glass dish in refrigerator 1 hour or more.

Drain marinade and discard. Cook chicken in a medium skillet or on a grill on medium heat until lightly browned and cooked through. Cool.

In a medium salad bowl, combine chicken, corn, black or kidney beans, jicama, green onions, avocado, and lettuce. Add amount of dressing desired. Sprinkle with Parmesan cheese and top with croutons, if desired.

Serves 4 to 6

GARDEN MACARONI SALAD

Include other garden vegetables in this salad, such as snap peas, carrots, radishes, and green beans.

FOR SALAD:

8	ounces shell macaroni or other pasta, cooked according to package directions, drained, and cooled
1	cup diced cucumber
1	cup diced tomatoes
2 to 3	green onions, chopped or ¼ cup chopped red onion

FOR DRESSING:

½	cup mayonnaise
1	tablespoon cider vinegar
1	teaspoon dried dill weed
1	teaspoon salt
¼	teaspoon pepper
1	teaspoon sugar

In a salad bowl, combine cooked macaroni, cucumber, tomatoes, and onion. Toss with dressing. Cover and chill for 1 hour before serving.

To make dressing, in a small bowl, mix mayonnaise, vinegar, dill weed, salt, pepper, and sugar.

Serves 4 to 6

Family Tip: Lure your family to the table with exciting new recipes. The Internet is a good source for new recipe ideas.

PASTA VEGETABLE SALAD

Any combination of vegetables makes a delicious salad. Vegetable amounts are approximate.

- 1 package (8 ounces) rotelle or spiral pasta, cooked according to package directions and drained
- ⅓ cup broccoli florets
- ⅓ cup cauliflower florets
- ⅓ cup thinly sliced or julienned carrots
- ⅓ cup diced green pepper
- ⅓ cup sliced red onion
- ⅓ cup diced tomatoes
- ⅓ cup sliced mushrooms
- ⅓ cup sliced cucumber or zucchini
- ⅓ cup sliced olives
- 1 bottle (8 ounces) Italian salad dressing (or less to taste)
- ½ cup grated mozzarella or cheddar cheese

Wash broccoli, cauliflower, carrots, and green pepper, leaving a little water on vegetables. Place in a microwave dish and microwave on high for 30 to 45 seconds to soften vegetables. Microwave red onion separately for 20 seconds. Do not microwave tomatoes, mushrooms, cucumber or zucchini, or olives.

Put cooked pasta in a large salad bowl. Add vegetables. Pour desired amount of dressing to coat. Store in the refrigerator an hour or more to blend flavors. Sprinkle cheese on salad just before serving.

Serves 6

Save Time: Buy baby carrots ready for use rather than peeling and cutting whole carrots.

CREAMY POPPY SEED DRESSING

Perfect for a fruit salad.

½   cup buttermilk
½   cup sour cream
2   tablespoons honey
1   tablespoon lemon juice
1   tablespoon poppy seeds

In a small bowl, whisk buttermilk, sour cream, honey, and lemon juice until smooth. Add poppy seeds and mix. Dressing can be stored in refrigerator up to 4 days.

Makes about 1 cup

BLEU CHEESE DRESSING

An exceptional dressing for any green salad.

⅓   cup mayonnaise
⅓   cup sour cream
1½   tablespoons red wine vinegar
2   tablespoons chopped green onions or shallot
⅔   cup crumbled bleu cheese
     Coarse salt to taste
     Freshly ground pepper to taste

In a medium bowl, mix mayonnaise, sour cream, vinegar, green onion or shallot, and bleu cheese. Add salt and pepper to taste. Serve over iceberg lettuce wedges or toss with a green salad.

Makes about 1 cup

CREAMY CILANTRO DRESSING

This refreshing dressing keeps in the refrigerator up to 2 weeks—that is, if you can keep it that long!

1	package ranch dressing mix
1	cup mayonnaise
½	cup buttermilk
1	cup minced cilantro
1	cup salsa verde
2	cloves garlic, minced
½ to 1	can (4 ounces) diced green chiles (to taste)
	Dash crushed red pepper flakes

In a large bowl, combine ranch dressing mix, mayonnaise, buttermilk, cilantro, salsa verde, garlic, and green chiles. Blend well. Add red pepper flakes to taste.

Makes 1 quart

Save Time: Don't chop or mince cilantro—just pull the leaves off the stems and use a little more than recipe calls for.

Breads

ORANGE ROLLS

So easy and so good!

1 to 2	tablespoons grated orange peel
⅓	cup butter
¾	cup sugar
2	tubes (12 ounces each) buttermilk biscuits

Heat oven to 350° F.

Mix orange peel, butter, and sugar in a saucepan over low heat until bubbly. Arrange biscuits sideways around a Bundt pan. Pour orange mixture over rolls.

Bake for 20 to 25 minutes. Invert rolls onto a platter.

Serves 6 to 8

POTATO REFRIGERATOR ROLLS

By having the dough waiting in your fridge, you can spoil your family any night with hot rolls for dinner.

1	cup mashed potatoes
¾	cup butter or margarine, softened
½	cup sugar
2	teaspoons salt
2	eggs
2	tablespoons yeast
½	cup warm water
1	teaspoon sugar
½	cup milk, scalded and cooled
7	cups flour
	Melted butter for brushing

Mix potatoes with butter, sugar, salt, and eggs in a large bowl or bread mixer. Dissolve yeast in water. Sprinkle 1 teaspoon sugar over top and let yeast activate a few minutes. Add milk and yeast to potato mixture. Beat for 2 minutes. Gradually stir in flour until stiff enough to knead. Knead on a lightly floured surface or in bread mixer, until smooth and elastic. Put dough into a greased bowl and turn dough to grease both sides. Cover and let rise until doubled in size.

Punch dough down. Place in a greased 2-quart casserole. Butter top of dough and cover with casserole lid. Place in refrigerator at least 24 hours. About 1 hour before baking, remove desired amount of dough and shape into rolls. Place on greased baking sheet; brush rolls with melted butter. Cover and let rise until doubled, about 1 hour.

Bake at 400° F for 15 to 20 minutes.

Dough will keep in refrigerator up to 1 week.

Makes 2½ dozen medium-size rolls

Homemade rolls make any dinner an occasion.

2	cups milk
½	cup shortening
½	cup sugar
1	cup lukewarm water
2	heaping tablespoons yeast
2	teaspoons sugar
2½	teaspoons salt
3	eggs, beaten
7 to 9	cups flour
½	cup butter, melted

In a medium saucepan, bring milk, shortening, and sugar to a boil. Cool to lukewarm.

In a large bowl or bread mixer, combine water, yeast, sugar, and salt. Let yeast activate about 10 minutes. Add milk mixture, eggs, and 1 cup flour. Beat until smooth. Add flour, a cup at a time, until dough pulls away from sides of the bowl, but is not stiff. Knead about 10 minutes.

Place dough in a greased bowl, turn over, and cover with plastic wrap sprayed with nonstick cooking spray. Let rise in a warm place until doubled, about 1 hour. Punch down; let rise again.

Divide dough in half and place one part on a floured board or counter. Roll to ½ inch thick. Cut with a biscuit cutter or drinking glass. Dip one side in melted butter and fold over. (Or roll into a large circle, cut into wedges, and roll into crescents.) Brush with butter.

Place rolls close together on a greased baking sheet. Let rise until doubled in size, about 1 hour.

Heat oven to 425° F. Bake for 12 to 15 minutes, until golden brown.

Makes about 3½ dozen rolls

OAT ROLLS

These rolls are great with a bowl of hot soup.

2	cups old-fashioned or quick-cooking oats
½	cup brown sugar
¼	cup butter, softened
1	tablespoon salt
2½	cups boiling water
2	tablespoons yeast
½	cup warm water
½	teaspoon sugar
5 to 6	cups flour
2	tablespoons butter, softened

In a large mixing bowl or bread mixer, combine oats, brown sugar, butter, and salt. Add boiling water and mix. Let cool to lukewarm.

In a small bowl, sprinkle yeast over warm water. Sprinkle with sugar. Let activate about 5 minutes. Add yeast mixture and 2 cups flour to oat mixture. Mix until smooth. Add enough flour, a cup at a time, to form a soft dough. If using a bread mixer, knead for 5 to 8 minutes. Or place dough on a floured surface and knead by hand 8 to 10 minutes. Place dough in a greased bowl, turning to grease top. Cover and let rise in a warm place until dough has doubled in size, about 1 hour.

Punch dough down. Divide into 20 balls. Place in a greased 9- x 13-inch cake pan. For larger rolls, divide into 16 balls and place in two 9-inch cake pans. Cover and let rise until doubled in size, about 45 minutes to 1 hour.

Heat oven to 350° F. Bake rolls for 35 to 40 minutes, until golden brown. Brush tops with butter. Cool on a wire rack.

Makes 16 or 20 rolls

WHEAT ROLLS

Slathered with homemade jam or honey butter, these rolls will be the star of the meal.

2	tablespoons active dry yeast
2	cups buttermilk, warmed but not hot
½	cup + ¼ cup melted butter, divided
½	cup honey
3 to 3½	cups whole wheat flour
1½	teaspoons salt
1	teaspoon baking soda
1½ to 2½	cups white flour

Dissolve yeast in buttermilk in a large bowl or the bowl of a bread mixer. Add ½ cup butter, honey, whole wheat flour, salt, and baking soda. Mix well. Add enough white flour to form a soft dough. Knead by hand or with bread mixer for 7 to 8 minutes until smooth and elastic. Put in a greased bowl, turning dough once to grease all sides. Cover with a damp towel or plastic wrap that has been sprayed with nonstick cooking spray and let rise in a warm place until double in size, for about 1 hour.

Punch down dough. Divide dough into golf-ball size pieces. Shape each into a ball. Place 2 inches apart on baking sheets that have been greased or sprayed with nonstick cooking spray. Cover and let rise until double in size, about 30 minutes.

Heat oven to 400° F. Brush rolls with ¼ cup melted butter and bake for 12 to 15 minutes, until golden brown. Cool on wire racks.

Serve with Honey Butter (see page 89).

Makes 3½ dozen rolls

YUMMY BUNS

A versatile recipe; dough can be made into buns, pizza, scones, or cinnamon rolls.

2	cups water
½	cup butter
2	tablespoons rapid-mix yeast
½	cup sugar
1	egg
2	teaspoons salt
4 to 5	cups flour
	Butter for finishing

Heat water in a pan on stovetop or in microwave and melt ½ cup butter in it. Cool until warm. Add yeast, sugar, egg, and salt. Mix in bread mixer or with electric beater. Add 3 cups flour and beat. Add remaining flour, a cup at a time, until a soft dough is formed. Knead dough for 8 to 10 minutes by hand or with bread mixer. Place in a greased bowl and cover with a damp towel. Let rise until doubled in size, about 2 hours.

Punch down and shape into buns or rolls. Let rise again.

Heat oven to 350° F. Bake rolls 12 to 15 minutes, until golden brown. Rub butter over the tops of buns or rolls when baked.

Makes 2 to 2½ dozen buns or rolls

Family Tip: Make dinner interesting by cooking the same foods you loved as a child and telling your own children about your favorite childhood memories.

ONION-HERB BATTER BREAD

Vary this bread with different herbs for exciting new tastes.

½	cup milk, scalded
1½	tablespoons + ½ teaspoon sugar, divided
1½	teaspoons butter
1	teaspoon salt
1	tablespoon yeast
½	cup warm water
2 to 2¼	cups flour
1	tablespoon dried minced onion
½	teaspoon dried dill weed, rosemary, or other herbs (or 2 to 3 tablespoons fresh herbs)
	Butter for finishing
	Coarse salt for finishing

To scalded milk, add 1½ tablespoons sugar, butter, and salt, stirring until dissolved. Cool to lukewarm. In a large bowl, sprinkle yeast in warm water; sprinkle with a ½ teaspoon sugar to help activate yeast. Allow yeast to develop for a few minutes. Add milk mixture, then flour. Add onions and herbs. Stir together until blended, about 2 minutes. Cover and let rise in a warm location until tripled in size, about 45 minutes. Stir down and beat vigorously for ½ minute.

Heat oven to 350° F. Turn dough into a sprayed or greased 8- or 9-inch cake pan. Bake about 1 hour. Remove bread from pan; rub top with butter, and then sprinkle with coarse salt. Cool on rack.

Serves 6

Save Time: Use kitchen shears for quickly cutting many foods, such as cutting meats and breads into cubes, trimming fat, or snipping herbs.

Biscuit mix makes this a very quick bread.

½   cup chopped onion
2   teaspoons olive oil
1½ cups biscuit mix
1   egg
½   cup milk
1   cup grated cheddar cheese, divided
2   teaspoons dried parsley flakes
1   tablespoon butter or margarine, melted

Heat oven to 400° F.

In a small skillet, sauté onion in olive oil until soft. In a medium bowl, combine biscuit mix, egg, and milk, stirring until just combined. Add onion, ½ cup cheese, and parsley.

Spread batter in an 8- or 9-inch round baking pan. Sprinkle with remaining ½ cup cheese. Drizzle with butter. Bake for 15 to 20 minutes, or until cheese is melted and top is golden brown.

Serves 6

Cooking Tip: To grate cheese more easily, place it in the freezer for 15 to 20 minutes before grating.

GARLIC CHEESE BREADSTICKS

Easy! Just remember to thaw bread dough ahead of time.

1   loaf (1 pound) frozen bread dough
½   cup butter or margarine
1   teaspoon garlic salt
⅓   cup Parmesan cheese (or to taste)

Heat oven to 375° F.

Thaw loaf of bread dough. Melt butter or margarine and mix with garlic salt (keep warm). Roll loaf out to ¼ inch thick or more, rolling with the length of the loaf. Cut lengthwise into 1-inch wide strips, and then cut the strips into quarters (or the length of breadsticks desired). Dip each strip into the garlic butter, making sure it is covered all over. Place strips in a 9- x 13-inch pan or on a baking sheet ¼-inch apart, stretching when placing. Sprinkle with Parmesan cheese and let rise for about ½ hour or until doubled in size. Bake for 10 minutes, or until golden brown.

Makes about 2½ dozen breadsticks

Save Time: Plan menus and prepare a shopping list for the menus, as well as items you regularly buy, before going to the grocery store so that you can make one trip to the store rather than several.

BREADSTICKS

Less than an hour from start to finish.

1	tablespoon yeast
1	tablespoon sugar
1½	cups warm water
1	teaspoon salt
3 to 4	cups flour
¼	cup butter or margarine, melted
	Garlic salt or coarse salt (optional)
	Rosemary or other herbs (optional)
	Parmesan cheese (optional)

In a large bowl, put yeast and sugar in warm water. Let yeast activate a few minutes. Add salt and 3 cups flour. Mix well. Add more flour if dough is too sticky to handle. Knead for 5 minutes.

Put melted butter or margarine in a 10- x 15-inch jelly roll pan. Sprinkle lightly with garlic salt or coarse salt, if desired. Roll dough ½ inch thick. Cut into 1-inch strips. Roll each piece in butter. (Or press dough onto pan and cut into strips with a pizza cutter.) Sprinkle with rosemary or other herbs and Parmesan cheese, if desired.

Heat oven to 375° F. Let breadsticks rise for 20 minutes, and then bake for 20 minutes.

Makes about 18 breadsticks

This dough also makes a terrific pizza crust.

- 2½ cups warm water
- 2 tablespoons sugar
- 1½ tablespoons rapid-mix yeast
- 3 teaspoons garlic salt
- 3 teaspoons Italian seasoning
- 2 tablespoons olive oil
- 6 cups flour
  - Olive oil for finishing
  - Coarse salt for finishing

In a large bowl, combine water, sugar, and yeast. Add garlic salt, Italian seasoning, and olive oil. Stirring with a wooden spoon, add flour in stages until dough is soft but not sticky. Remove from bowl and place on a floured surface. Knead for a few minutes.

Grease a 12- x 15-inch baking sheet or spray with nonstick cooking spray. Spread dough on baking sheet. Let rise for 30 minutes. Lightly push fingers into dough at intervals. Brush a small amount of olive oil over bread to coat, and then sprinkle lightly with coarse salt.

Bake at 425° F for 15 to 20 minutes, until lightly browned on top.

Serves 12 to 15

Save Money: Purchase plastic wrap in large rolls at discount stores. Cover leftovers in refrigerator to use for another meal.

FRENCH BREAD

Make two loaves of fresh-from-the-oven French bread—one for your family and one for a friend.

2 tablespoons dry yeast
½ cup warm water
6 cups flour
2 cups hot water
5 tablespoons vegetable or olive oil
3 tablespoons sugar
1 tablespoon salt
1 egg white, beaten
Sesame seeds (optional)

Dissolve yeast in ½ cup warm water. Let activate for 10 minutes. In the bowl of a bread mixer or a mixer with a dough hook, blend 3 cups flour, hot water, oil, sugar, and salt. Add yeast mixture. Mix well, about 3 to 4 minutes. Add remaining flour, a cup at a time, until dough pulls away from the sides of the bowl. Mix well. Allow to rest for 10 minutes. Beat well. Rest again for 10 minutes. Beat well. Rest again for 10 minutes.

Heat oven to 350° F. Remove dough from bowl and place onto a floured counter or bread board. Divide dough in half. Shape each into an elongated loaf. (Or roll each half into a rectangle and roll up loosely jelly-roll style, and then seal the seam.) Place both loaves, seam side down, on a baking sheet that has been greased or sprayed with nonstick cooking spray. With a sharp knife, cut several diagonal slashes on the top of each loaf. Brush with egg white and sprinkle with sesame seeds, if desired. Cover with plastic wrap sprayed with nonstick cooking spray. Let rise 30 to 60 minutes. Bake for 30 minutes, until golden brown. Remove from oven and cool on a wire rack.

Makes 2 loaves

CHEESY FRENCH BREAD

This French bread will disappear in a hurry.

½	cup grated sharp cheddar cheese
½	cup grated Parmesan cheese
½	cup mayonnaise
2 to 3	green onions, chopped
1	loaf French bread, sliced

In a small bowl, mix cheddar cheese, Parmesan cheese, and mayonnaise. Add green onions. Spread on slices of French bread. Broil until cheese melts and is bubbly.

Serves 8 to 10

FRENCH BREAD WITH ONION SPREAD

Instead of butter and garlic on French bread, try this easy onion spread.

¼	cup olive oil
2	onions, finely chopped
1	tablespoon sugar
2	tablespoons balsamic or red wine vinegar
1	loaf French bread, sliced
	Grated Parmesan cheese (optional)

In a small skillet, heat oil and sauté onion with sugar until browned and tender. Add vinegar, stirring to deglaze pan.

Heat oven to 350° F. Arrange bread slices on a baking sheet. Toast bread until golden brown, watching so that it doesn't burn. Spread onion mixture on each slice. Sprinkle with Parmesan, if desired. Return to oven briefly to melt cheese.

Serves 8 to 10

WHITE BREAD

"Sponging," which you will do in this recipe, creates lighter bread and reduces kneading time.

10 to 12	cups flour*
2	tablespoons rapid-mix yeast
4	cups warm water
⅓	cup vegetable oil
⅓	cup sugar or honey
1	tablespoon salt

Put 6 cups flour into bread mixer or a mixer bowl equipped with a dough hook. Add yeast. Pulse to mix well. Add water and mix about 1 minute. Cover bowl, and let dough rest, or "sponge," for 10 minutes.

Add oil, sugar or honey, and salt. Add remaining flour, a cup at a time, mixing until dough pulls away from the sides of the bowl. The amount of flour may vary. Mix at medium speed 8 to 10 minutes. If kneading by hand, knead for 12 to 15 minutes, until dough is smooth and elastic.

Heat oven to 350° F. Lightly oil hands and counter or cutting board. Divide dough into 3 equal portions. Shape into loaves and place in 5- x 9-inch loaf pans that have been greased or sprayed with nonstick cooking spray. Cover bread with a damp towel or plastic wrap that has been sprayed with nonstick cooking spray. Let dough rise until double, about 30 to 60 minutes. (Rising time will vary depending on warmth of kitchen.) Bake for about 30 minutes, until crust is golden brown. Remove from pans and let cool on wire racks.

Makes 3 loaves

*Note: Whole wheat flour or a combination of white and whole wheat flour may be used in this recipe. Adding a dough enhancer or high-gluten flour to whole wheat flour adds volume and improves texture. Follow directions on package.

BISCUITS

Much quicker to make than rolls, hot biscuits out of the oven will be snatched right up.

2 cups flour
3 teaspoons baking powder
½ teaspoon salt
½ teaspoon cream of tartar
½ cup chilled butter, cut in pieces
⅔ cup milk
3 teaspoons honey

In a large bowl, mix flour, baking powder, salt, and cream of tartar. With a pastry blender or fork, cut in butter until mixture resembles coarse crumbs. Add milk and honey, mixing until just blended. Knead on a floured surface 8 to 10 times.

Heat oven to 450° F. Roll out dough to ¾ inch thick. Cut in circles with a 2½-inch biscuit cutter or drinking glass. Place at least 1 inch apart on a baking sheet that has been greased or sprayed with nonstick cooking spray. Bake for 10 to 12 minutes, or until light brown.

Makes 8 large biscuits

PARMESAN BISCUITS

These family favorites can be ready in minutes!

- 3 tablespoons grated Parmesan cheese
- 1 teaspoon onion powder or ½ teaspoon garlic powder
- 1 tube (12 ounces) refrigerator biscuits

Heat oven to 400° F.

Put Parmesan cheese and onion powder or garlic powder in a resealable plastic bag. Cut each biscuit in half. Drop several biscuit pieces at a time in bag and shake to coat. Place biscuits on a greased baking sheet. Bake for 8 to 9 minutes, or until golden brown.

Serves 4 to 6

Family Tip: Hold family reunions, whether for an afternoon or a weekend, to gather extended family members. Make it potluck so that preparing food for a crowd is easy. Encourage mingling through games, sports, conversation, sharing memories, and service projects. Have mixed seating at dinner tables so that individual families do not all bunch together.

Corn bread complements a multitude of soups, salads, and main courses.

⅓	cup butter or margarine, melted
¼	cup honey
2	eggs
1	cup buttermilk
½	teaspoon baking soda
1	cup corn meal
1	cup flour
1	teaspoon salt

Heat oven to 350° F.

In a small bowl, mix butter and honey together. Blend in eggs. Measure buttermilk in a glass cup and add baking soda. In a large bowl, mix corn meal, flour, and salt together. Fold in butter-honey mixture and buttermilk mixture. Stir until just moistened.

Spoon corn bread into a 9-inch square pan that has been greased or sprayed with nonstick cooking spray. Bake for 30 minutes.

Serves 6 to 9

FLOUR TORTILLAS

Hot and buttered, these tortillas are a favorite food for kids.
Store extras in a covered container or plastic bag and reheat on
a hot griddle.

3	cups flour
1½	teaspoons baking powder
1	teaspoon salt
1½	cups warm water
1	tablespoon oil or shortening

Stir together flour, baking powder, and salt in a large mixing bowl. Add water, a little at a time, mixing with dry ingredients until dough is very soft dough but not sticky. If after kneading a few minutes it feels too wet, add a little more flour. Add oil or shortening and knead until dough is soft and satin-like. Cover and let rest while griddle or skillet heats over medium-high heat.

Make 12 dough balls, each a little larger than a golf ball. Roll tortillas into about 5- to 6-inch rounds. Use a heavy, weighted rolling pin for easier rolling. Roll tortilla very thin, less than ⅛ inch thick. Spray a griddle or skillet with nonstick cooking spray or grease with oil. Cook tortillas until bubbles come through to top. Turn over and cook until done.

Makes 12 tortillas

Family Tip: As a family, prepare a meal to share with someone—a neighbor, someone who is ill, or anyone who would benefit from a thoughtful gesture.

SCONES

Frozen dough is a handy shortcut to freshly cooked scones. Served hot, these scones will disappear as fast as you can cook them.

Vegetable oil
12 frozen dinner rolls, thawed (or favorite bread or roll recipe)

Pour enough vegetable oil (about 1 to 2 inches) in an electric skillet to allow scones to cook without touching bottom of pan. Heat oil to 375° F.

Form scones by stretching or rolling individual thawed rolls into 3- to 4-inch circles. Using tongs, carefully place scones in hot oil. Cook until golden brown on one side; turn over and cook on other side. Drain on paper towels. Serve with fruit butter, honey butter, honey, or dusted with powdered sugar.

FRUIT BUTTER

½ cup butter (no substitutes), softened
1 cup fresh or frozen berries (strawberries, raspberries, blackberries, and/or Marionberries)

In a food processor or blender, blend butter and berries until smooth.

HONEY BUTTER

½ cup butter, softened
¼ cup honey
1 teaspoon vanilla

In a small bowl, beat together butter, honey, and vanilla until well mixed and smooth.

Serves 4 to 6

APPLE MUFFINS

Apples, cinnamon, and sugar—an unbeatable combination.

FOR MUFFINS:

¼ cup butter, softened
½ cup sugar
1 egg
1½ cups flour
½ teaspoon salt
½ teaspoon cinnamon
3 teaspoons baking powder
½ cup milk
1 cup peeled and grated apples

FOR TOPPING:

½ cup brown sugar
⅓ cup chopped walnuts or pecans
½ teaspoon cinnamon

Heat oven to 375° F.

In a large bowl, cream together butter and sugar. Add egg and blend well. In a separate bowl, sift or stir together flour, salt, cinnamon, and baking powder. Add to butter mixture. Add milk and apples. Stir until moistened.

Grease or spray muffin cups with nonstick cooking spray, or use cupcake liners. Fill each cup ⅔ full with batter. Sprinkle topping on muffin batter. Bake for 25 minutes, or until golden.

For topping, in a small bowl, mix together brown sugar, nuts, and cinnamon.

Makes 12 muffins

BLUEBERRY MUFFINS

Buy fresh blueberries when they're at a good price, then freeze some. You'll have large, luscious berries to add to many recipes, including salads, desserts, or these better-than-bakery muffins.

FOR MUFFINS:

½	cup butter or margarine, softened
1	cup sugar
2	eggs
¾	cup sour cream
1	teaspoon vanilla
1⅓	cups flour
½	teaspoon salt
2	teaspoons baking powder
1 to 1½	cups frozen blueberries (leave frozen)

FOR TOPPING:

¼	cup butter or margarine, softened
3 to 4	tablespoons flour
3	tablespoons brown sugar
3	tablespoons sugar
¼	cup chopped pecans

Heat oven to 375° F.

Cream butter and sugar in a large bowl. Add eggs, sour cream, and vanilla. Mix well. Add flour, salt, and baking powder. Stir only until mixed. Gently fold in blueberries. Grease or spray muffin cups with nonstick cooking spray, or use cupcake liners. Fill ⅔ full with batter. Sprinkle topping over muffin batter. Bake for 25 to 30 minutes.

For topping, mix butter, flour, brown sugar, sugar, and pecans in a small bowl.

Makes 12 muffins

BRAN MUFFINS

Whole-grain goodness! Serve a basket of these muffins with dinner and save a few for breakfast.

2	cups bran flakes
1	cup milk
½	cup brown sugar
½	cup vegetable oil
½	cup honey
3	eggs
1	cup flour
½	teaspoon salt
1	teaspoon baking soda
¾	cup raisins

Heat oven to 400° F.

In a large bowl, combine bran flakes, milk, brown sugar, oil, honey, eggs, flour, salt, and baking soda. With an electric mixer on medium speed, blend until well mixed, about 5 minutes. Stir in raisins.

Grease or spray muffin cups with nonstick cooking spray, or use cupcake liners. Fill muffin cups ⅔ full. Bake for 18 to 20 minutes.

Makes 1½ dozen medium muffins

CHEESE MUFFINS

Favorite cheeses such as Swiss, cheddar, Monterey Jack, or Provolone can be used to make these muffins.

2	cups sifted flour
4	teaspoons baking powder
1	tablespoon sugar
½	teaspoon salt
1	egg
1	cup milk
3	tablespoons butter, melted
1	cup (or more, if desired) cheddar or other cheese, grated

Heat oven to 350° F.

Mix flour, baking powder, sugar, and salt into a large bowl. Combine egg, milk, and butter in a small bowl. Add egg mixture to flour mixture. Add cheese. Stir until moistened. Grease or spray muffin cups with nonstick cooking spray, or use cupcake liners. Fill muffin cups ⅔ full with batter. Bake for 15 to 20 minutes, until golden brown.

Makes 1 dozen muffins

SPICE MUFFINS

Experiment a little by adding nuts, raisins, or dried cranberries to these marvelous muffins.

FOR MUFFINS:

2   cups flour
2   teaspoons baking powder
¼   teaspoon salt
2   teaspoons cinnamon
¾   cup sugar
1   cup milk
1   egg
1   teaspoon grated orange peel
⅓   cup butter, melted

FOR TOPPING:

¼   cup sugar
½   teaspoon cinnamon
1   tablespoon butter, melted
1   tablespoon flour
⅓   cup chopped pecans or walnuts

Heat oven to 375° F.

In a large bowl, stir together flour, baking powder, salt, cinnamon, and sugar. In a small bowl, combine milk, egg, orange peel, and butter. Add egg mixture to flour mixture, stirring until just combined.

Grease or spray muffin cups with nonstick cooking spray, or use cupcake liners. Fill cups about ⅔ full. Sprinkle with topping. Bake for 18 to 20 minutes.

For topping, combine sugar, cinnamon, butter, flour, and nuts in a small bowl.

Makes 1 dozen muffins

Beef

SLOW-COOKER POT ROAST

Put this roast on in the morning, and the aroma will greet your family when they come home for dinner.

1	beef roast (4 to 5 pounds—chuck, rump, blade, tip, or eye of round)
2	large onions, sliced
2	cups baby carrots
6 to 8	potatoes, peeled and quartered
¾	cup ketchup
⅓	cup red wine vinegar
2	tablespoons Worcestershire sauce
1½	teaspoons salt
½	cup water
1	tablespoon dried rosemary or 3 tablespoons fresh rosemary

Trim fat from roast and place in a large slow cooker. Add onions, carrots, and potatoes.

In a medium bowl, mix ketchup, vinegar, Worcestershire sauce, salt, and water. Pour over roast and vegetables. Sprinkle with rosemary. Cook roast on low heat for 8 to 10 hours, or medium-to-high heat for 4 to 5 hours.

Serves 6 to 8

Save Money: Use less expensive cuts of beef, such round steak or chuck blade roast. Cook them for several hours with low, moist heat or marinate to tenderize the meat.

MARINATED ROAST BEEF

Make gravy with the flavorful meat juices and serve over mashed potatoes or rice.

- 1   cup soy sauce
- ¾   cup brown sugar
- 1   cup water
- ⅔   cup cider vinegar
- ½   teaspoon ground ginger
- ½   teaspoon garlic powder
- 1   roast (3 to 4 pounds—rump, tip, chuck, eye of round, cross-rib, or blade)
- 2   tablespoons cornstarch or flour
- ¼   cup water

In a medium bowl, mix together soy sauce, brown sugar, water, vinegar, ginger, and garlic powder. Put mixture into a large resealable plastic bag or covered glass dish. Put roast in bag or dish and marinate in the refrigerator overnight, turning several times.

Place roast and marinade in a slow cooker and cook for 8 to 9 hours on low heat. Remove roast from slow cooker. In a small bowl, mix cornstarch or flour with water until smooth. Add to meat juices. Cook on high for about 10 minutes, or until thickened.

Serves 6 to 8

Save Time: Keep a jar of an equal mixture of flour and cornstarch. Place 3 or 4 tablespoons of this mixture in another jar and add some water. Shake well for a smooth paste to thicken gravy.

POT ROAST WITH HOMEMADE NOODLES

Homemade noodles are easy to make and with this roast are a sure family favorite.

FOR ROAST:

	Salt and pepper to taste
1	chuck or pot roast (3 to 4 pounds)
1	large onion, chopped
2	tablespoons olive oil
1	cup water
1	can (14 ounces) beef broth
2	cups water

FOR NOODLES:

1	cup flour
¾	teaspoon salt
1	egg
2½	tablespoons milk

Salt and pepper roast. In a roast pan or Dutch oven, brown roast and onion in olive oil. Add 1 cup water. Cover pan and bake at 325° F for 2½ to 3 hours, until meat is tender.

When the roast is nearly cooked, make noodles. Combine flour and salt in a bowl, making a well in the center. Beat egg and milk and pour into well. Stir to form a stiff dough. Put mixture on a well-floured surface and roll into a thin, large rectangle, about 12 x 15 inches. With a sharp knife, cut into ¼-inch strips, or use a pasta machine.

Remove roast from cooking pan; cover to keep warm. Add beef broth and 2 cups water to pan. Bring to a boil; then add noodles. Cook for 8 to 10 minutes or until tender. Drain. Serve with roast.

Serves 6 to 8

SALSA BEEF

Salsa and cilantro add zest to roast beef.

1   boneless shoulder or rump roast (2 to 3 pounds)
1   tablespoon olive oil
1   cup medium salsa
2   tablespoons brown sugar
1   tablespoon soy sauce
1   teaspoon minced garlic
3   tablespoons chopped cilantro
1   tablespoon lime juice
3   cups hot cooked rice

Trim fat from beef and cut into 2-inch cubes. Heat olive oil in a large covered pot or Dutch oven and brown meat. Pour off drippings. Add salsa, brown sugar, soy sauce, and garlic. Bring to a boil; then reduce heat to low. Cover and simmer 1 hour or longer. Remove lid and continue cooking for an additional 30 minutes. Remove beef from heat and add cilantro and lime juice. Stir. Serve over cooked rice.

Serves 4 to 6

Save Money: Plan meals and grocery shop with a list of needed items. Avoid buying on impulse.

SLOPPY JOES

Teenagers will quickly gobble these up.

2	pounds ground beef
¾	cup chopped onion
¾	cup chopped celery
1	teaspoon vinegar
1	teaspoon Worcestershire sauce
1	cup ketchup
1	cup water
2	tablespoons flour
2	tablespoons brown sugar
8 to 10	hamburger buns or sandwich rolls

Brown ground beef with onion and celery in a large skillet. Add vinegar, Worcestershire sauce, ketchup, and water. Add flour and brown sugar. Simmer for 20 to 30 minutes. Serve on buns or rolls.

Serves 8 to 10

Save Time: Instead of cooking meatballs in a skillet on top of the stove, where you have to turn them one at a time, place them on a greased broiler pan and bake at 350° F for 20 to 25 minutes. Rather than rolling meatballs, just cut ground beef in 1-inch cubes.

SHEPHERD'S PIE

Shepherd's Pie is an old favorite for many families.

1	pound ground beef
1	small onion, chopped
½	teaspoon salt
½	teaspoon pepper
1	can (15 ounces) tomato sauce or 1 can (10¾ ounces) tomato soup
1	can (16 ounces) green beans, drained
½	teaspoon basil
6 to 8	potatoes, cooked, drained, and mashed
½ to 1	cup grated cheddar cheese
	Paprika

Heat oven to at 350° F.

Cook ground beef and onion in a large skillet until beef is browned. Add salt and pepper. Add tomato sauce or soup, beans, and basil and simmer for 5 minutes. Place meat in a greased or sprayed 3-quart casserole or 10-inch pie pan. Spread mashed potatoes over meat, sprinkle with cheese and a few shakes of paprika. Bake for 20 minutes, uncovered, or until heated thoroughly.

Serves 4 to 6

CREAMY SHEPHERD'S PIE

Instead of a tomato base, this shepherd's pie has a cream soup base, giving it an altogether different flavor.

1 to 1½	pounds ground beef
1	onion, chopped
½	teaspoon salt
¼	teaspoon pepper
1	can (10¾ ounces) cream of mushroom soup
½	soup can milk
6 to 8	potatoes, cooked, drained, and mashed
½ to 1	cup grated cheese

Heat oven to 350° F.

Mix ground beef with onion, salt, and pepper in a medium bowl. In a small bowl, mix mushroom soup with milk and add half of this mixture to ground beef. Put meat mixture in a greased or sprayed 9- or 10-inch glass pie plate or a 3-quart casserole. Bake, uncovered, for 25 to 30 minutes or microwave on high for 10 minutes until cooked through, stirring several times. Spoon off grease. Add remaining mushroom soup and milk mixture to potatoes. Blend thoroughly. Spread mashed potatoes over meat and sprinkle with cheese. Return to oven or microwave and heat until potatoes are hot and cheese is melted.

Serves 4 to 6

Family Tip: To get to know each other better, play family trivia games at the dinner table. Prepare questions ahead of time or make them up as you go. Ask questions, such as how long have Mom and Dad been married? What is (fill in the blank)'s favorite dessert? Where would (fill in the blank) like to go on a dream vacation?

TACO CASSEROLE

One family member can prepare this dish in a matter of minutes while another sets the table and another makes a salad.

1	pound ground beef
1	can (8 ounces) tomato sauce
1	can (15 ounces) kidney beans, drained and rinsed, or refried beans
1	small can (2¼ ounces) sliced black olives (optional)
½ to 1	cup grated cheddar cheese
1	package (16 ounces) Fritos

Brown ground beef in a medium skillet or put in a glass dish, break in pieces, and microwave on high for 4 to 5 minutes. Combine ground beef with tomato sauce, beans, and olives, if desired, and put into a 2- or 3-quart casserole. Heat in microwave on high until thoroughly heated, about 2 to 3 minutes. Sprinkle with cheese. Serve over Fritos.

Serves 4 to 5

Save Time: Make one-dish or one-skillet meals, thus reducing preparation and cleanup time.

TACO STUFFED PEPPERS

These stuffed peppers are a new variation on an old theme.

¾ to 1   pound ground beef
1   envelope (1½ ounces) taco seasoning mix
¾   cup water
1   can (15 ounces) kidney beans, rinsed and drained
1   cup salsa
2   quarts water
4   large bell peppers
1   tomato, chopped
½   cup grated cheddar cheese
½   cup sour cream

Heat oven to 350° F.

Brown ground beef in a large skillet. Drain grease. Add taco seasoning mix, ¾ cup water, kidney beans, and salsa. Mix well. Bring to a boil over medium-high heat. Reduce heat and simmer, uncovered, for 5 minutes to blend flavors.

Heat 2 quarts water to boiling in a large saucepan. Cut peppers in half lengthwise and remove seeds. Place peppers in boiling water and cook for 3 minutes. Remove and drain. Arrange pepper halves in an ungreased baking dish. Divide ground beef mixture among the halves (about ½ cup in each). Cover dish with aluminum foil and bake for 15 to 20 minutes, until peppers are tender but crisp and filling is heated through. Top each serving with chopped tomatoes, cheese, and sour cream.

Serves 4 to 6

Family Tip: Special occasions are wonderful opportunities to bring families together. Graduations, birthdays, anniversaries, and weddings are events that can be made memorable with family dinners.

MEXICAN LASAGNA

A new twist on an old family favorite.

1½	pounds ground beef
1	envelope (1½ ounces) taco seasoning mix
½ to 1	teaspoon seasoned salt
1	cup diced tomatoes (fresh or canned)
2	cans (8 ounces each) tomato sauce
1	can (4 ounces) diced green chiles (more, if desired)
1	cup ricotta cheese
2	eggs, beaten
6 to 8	corn tortillas, cut in 2-inch strips
2½	cups grated Monterey Jack cheese

Heat oven to 350° F.

In a large skillet, brown ground beef. Drain grease. Add taco seasoning mix, seasoned salt, tomatoes, tomato sauce, and chiles. Simmer, uncovered, 10 minutes. In a small bowl, combine ricotta cheese and eggs.

Spray a 9- x 13-inch baking pan with nonstick cooking spray. Spread half of meat mixture in pan; lay half of tortilla strips over meat. Spread half of ricotta cheese mixture on top of this, and then sprinkle with half of Monterey Jack cheese. Repeat layers. Bake for 30 minutes, or until cheese is melted and lightly browned. Let stand 10 minutes before serving.

Serves 8

Save Time: Seasoned ground beef is the main ingredient in many recipes, such as chili, soups, tacos, and various casseroles. Cook several pounds of ground beef mixed with onions and seasonings at once. Store in the freezer for later use.

STIR-FRY BEEF WITH GINGER SAUCE

This recipe is also good with other vegetables, such as snow peas, thinly sliced carrots, zucchini, green pepper, and celery.

⅓	cup soy sauce
2	cups water
2	teaspoons brown sugar
2	tablespoons honey
1	teaspoon grated fresh ginger
¼	teaspoon pepper
1	teaspoon chicken bouillon granules
3	tablespoons cornstarch, dissolved in 1½ tablespoons water
1	tablespoon sesame oil
1	tablespoon olive oil
¾ to 1	pound sirloin steak, cut across grain in ½-inch strips
1½	cups broccoli florets
1	cup small button mushrooms or sliced mushrooms
1	tablespoon toasted sesame seeds
4 to 5	cups hot cooked rice

Combine soy sauce, water, brown sugar, honey, ginger, pepper, and bouillon in a medium saucepan. Bring to a boil; reduce heat. Add cornstarch dissolved in water and cook until sauce thickens, about 3 to 4 minutes. Keep warm.

In a large skillet or wok, heat sesame oil and olive oil. Cook steak strips in hot oils until browned on all sides and cooked through. Add broccoli and mushrooms and cook for a few minutes. Add 1 to 2 tablespoons water. Cover skillet and cook until broccoli is crisp-tender. Add sauce and bring to a simmer. Remove from heat and sprinkle with sesame seeds. Serve over rice.

Serves 4

Cooking Tip: To thinly slice meat for stir-fry dishes, first partially freeze meat. This allows you to slice it more easily and quickly.

FAJITAS

Give your family their choice of beef or chicken fajitas or cook smaller amounts of each.

1	can (6 ounces) frozen limeade concentrate, thawed
⅓	cup olive oil
⅓	cup lemon-lime soda
2	tablespoons red wine vinegar
½	teaspoon garlic powder
½	teaspoon chili powder
½	teaspoon cumin
¼	teaspoon salt
¼	teaspoon pepper
½ to 1	pound flank or sirloin steak, cut in strips OR 3 boneless, skinless chicken breasts, cut in strips
1	medium onion, sliced
1	medium green pepper, sliced
1	medium yellow or red pepper, sliced
1	tablespoon olive oil
8 to 12	flour tortillas
	Salsa (for serving)
	Sour cream (for serving)
	Lettuce, shredded (for serving)
	Cheddar or Mexican blend cheese, grated (for serving)

In a small bowl, combine limeade, olive oil, lemon-lime soda, vinegar, garlic powder, chili powder, cumin, salt, and pepper. Put beef or chicken in a plastic resealable bag. Add marinade. Marinate in refrigerator for 4 to 6 hours.

In a large skillet, cook beef or chicken until cooked through. (If cooking both kinds of meat, use separate skillets). In another skillet, sauté onion, green pepper, and yellow or red pepper in 1 tablespoon olive oil. Warm tortillas in oven or microwave. Put steak or chicken in center of tortilla and add salsa, sour cream, lettuce, and cheese as desired.

Serves 4 to 6 (2 fajitas per serving)

ORIENTAL STEAK ROLLS

These steak rolls are elegant in appearance, but easy to prepare.

1	pound flank steak
	Salt and pepper
16	asparagus spears, trimmed
16	thin green onions, trimmed
1	green pepper, cut in strips
16	mushrooms (any variety), sliced
1	carrot, julienned or thinly sliced
⅓	cup seasoned rice vinegar
⅓	cup soy sauce
3	teaspoons sugar
1	tablespoon sesame oil
½	tablespoon cornstarch

Slice steak across the grain into 16 strips, about ¼ inch thick (or have it sliced by butcher). Pound each piece very thin. Season with salt and pepper. Place an asparagus spear, green onion, slice of green pepper, and several mushroom and carrot slices on each piece of steak. Roll steak around vegetables and fasten with a toothpick. Place in a shallow glass baking dish.

Combine vinegar, soy sauce, sugar, and sesame oil. Pour over steak rolls. Marinate ½ hour. Drain marinade into a small saucepan.

Broil steak rolls 5 minutes per side, or until desired doneness. While steak is broiling, bring marinade to a boil. Mix cornstarch with a little water and add to marinade. Cook until slightly thickened. Serve over steak rolls.

Serves 6 to 8

FRENCH DIP SANDWICHES

Perfect for a Saturday supper. Put the roast in a slow cooker and head off for tennis, skiing, or bike riding, then come home to the enticing aroma of this meal.

1	boneless beef roast (2½ to 3 pounds, any kind—eye of round, chuck, cross-rib, rump)
2	cups water
½	cup soy sauce
1	teaspoon dried rosemary or 1 tablespoon fresh rosemary
½	teaspoon thyme
1	bay leaf
4	whole peppercorns
6 to 8	hard rolls or hoagie buns

Put roast in a slow cooker. In a small bowl, mix water, soy sauce, rosemary, thyme, bay leaf, and peppercorns. Pour over roast. Cover and cook on high heat for about 5 to 6 hours. Remove roast from pot and shred with 2 forks.

Strain broth, removing bay leaf and peppercorns. Serve hot broth in individual bowls or cups to dip sandwiches.

Serve 6 to 8

BARBECUED BEEF

Use your favorite bottle of barbecue sauce or try a new kind.

1	roast (3½ to 4 pounds, any kind)
1	bottle (18 ounces) barbecue sauce
1	small onion, chopped
1	clove garlic, minced
½	teaspoon pepper
10 to 12	sandwich or hamburger buns

Put roast, barbecue sauce, onion, garlic, and pepper in a slow cooker. Cook on low for 6 to 7 hours until meat is very tender. Remove meat from pot and shred with 2 forks. Return to sauce and mix. Serve on buns.

Serves 10 to 12

Family Tip: Build traditions around some of the less-celebrated holidays. With planning, any occasion can become a family tradition or a celebration. For example, have an Irish dinner on St. Patrick's Day. Eat corned beef, boiled cabbage, and Irish soda bread; or for a twist, eat only items that are green.

GOULASH

Goulash in Hungary is actually soup—but this Americanized recipe is thicker, like stew.

¼	cup butter or margarine
1	onion, chopped
1	clove garlic, minced
2	pounds beef cubes (chuck or round)
1	tablespoon Worcestershire sauce
1	can (8 ounces) tomato sauce or 1 cup canned tomatoes
2	tablespoons brown sugar
2	teaspoons salt
2	teaspoons paprika
½	teaspoon dry mustard
⅛	teaspoon cayenne pepper
1½	cups water
1	cup sliced celery
1	cup sliced carrots
1	small green pepper, chopped
2	tablespoons flour
¼	cup water
12 or 16	ounces egg noodles, cooked according to package directions

Melt butter in a large pot or Dutch oven. Sauté onion and garlic. Brown beef cubes. Add Worcestershire sauce, tomato sauce or tomatoes, brown sugar, salt, paprika, mustard, cayenne pepper, and 1½ cups water. Bring to a boil; reduce heat and simmer for 2 to 2 ½ hours.

Add celery, carrots, and green pepper; simmer another hour.

Before serving, blend flour and ¼ cup water. Stir flour mixture slowly into stew. Heat again to boiling, stirring constantly, until mixture is thickened, about 2 to 4 minutes. Serve over noodles.

Serves 6 to 8

BEEF TENDERLOIN WITH MUSHROOMS

Tenderloin, the most tender cut of beef, is excellent when dressed up with a flavorful sauce.

2	teaspoons olive oil
½	cup butter, divided
4	beef tenderloin steaks (1 inch thick)
1	cup sliced mushrooms
3	tablespoons chopped green onions
1½	tablespoons flour
¼	teaspoon salt
¼	teaspoon pepper
1¼	cups beef broth

In a large skillet, heat oil and ¼ cup butter over medium-high heat. Cook tenderloins 8 to 9 minutes per side, or until meat is cooked to desired doneness. Place on a serving platter, cover, and keep warm. To pan juices, add mushrooms, onions, and remaining butter. Sauté until soft; add flour, salt and pepper. Gradually stir in broth. Bring to a boil, cooking until sauce is slightly thickened. Return steak to pan to heat thoroughly. Serve mushroom sauce over steaks.

Serves 4

BEEF TENDERLOIN WITH MUSTARD SAUCE

Serve this beef tenderloin with Potato Cakes (see page 222) for a fabulous gourmet dinner. Cornichons are French pickles, available in most grocery stores or specialty stores. They are worth tracking down.

2½ to 3	pounds beef tenderloin
	Salt and pepper
2	tablespoons olive oil
1	cup white grape or apple juice
2	shallots, minced
2	teaspoons dried tarragon
8 to 10	cornichons (French pickles), sliced lengthwise in quarters
1	tablespoon cream
2	tablespoons butter
2	tablespoons Dijon mustard
3	teaspoons minced fresh tarragon

Heat oven to 450° F.

Season tenderloin with salt and pepper. Heat olive oil in an ovenproof skillet or roasting pan. Brown tenderloin on all sides. Roast tenderloin, uncovered, in oven for 30 to 35 minutes, or until a meat thermometer reaches 130° for medium-rare. Transfer tenderloin to a platter and cover with foil.

Using hot pads, place skillet or roasting pan with drippings on stovetop. Add grape juice, shallots, and dried tarragon. Bring to a boil, stirring up brown bits from roasting. Reduce liquid to about ½ cup and then add cornichons, cream, and any meat juices from platter. Turn heat to low and stir in butter, mustard, and fresh tarragon. Season with more salt and pepper to taste.

Slice tenderloin and serve with sauce.

Serves 4 to 6

RIB-EYE STEAKS

Serve rib-eye steaks for an elegant dinner. This recipe takes only minutes to prepare.

4	rib-eye steaks, ½ inch thick
½	teaspoon salt
¼	teaspoon pepper
4	tablespoons butter, divided
3	tablespoons finely chopped green onions
½	teaspoon dry mustard
1	tablespoon lemon juice
1½	teaspoons Worcestershire sauce
1	tablespoon minced fresh parsley
1	tablespoon minced fresh chives

Sprinkle steaks with salt and pepper. Melt 2 tablespoons butter in a large skillet. Cook onions and mustard for 1 minute. Add steaks, cooking on medium heat for 4 to 5 minutes on each side, or until meat is cooked to desired doneness. Remove to a serving platter. Add remaining 2 tablespoons butter, lemon juice, and Worcestershire sauce to skillet. Cook for 2 minutes; add parsley and chives. Serve sauce over steaks.

Serves 4

MEXICAN STEAK

A perky south-of-the border flavor.

1	pound round steak
1	medium onion, chopped
2	tablespoons butter
1½	teaspoons salt
¼	teaspoon chili powder
	Dash cayenne pepper
1	clove garlic, minced
¼	teaspoon cinnamon
¼	teaspoon celery seed
2	tablespoons prepared mustard
1	cup water
4 to 6	cups hot cooked rice

Cut steak into strips, about ½-inch x 2 inches. In a large skillet, sauté onion in butter until soft. Add steak and brown. Add salt, chili powder, cayenne pepper, garlic, cinnamon, celery seed, mustard, and water, stirring to mix. Bring to a boil, reduce heat, and cover. Simmer for 1 hour or longer. Serve over rice.

Serves 4 to 6

SLOW-COOKER SWISS STEAK

Fork-tender and very flavorful.

½ cup flour
1 teaspoon salt
½ teaspoon paprika
2 to 3 pounds round steak, cut in serving-size pieces
2 tablespoons olive or vegetable oil
1 large green pepper, thinly sliced
1 can (8 ounces) mushrooms, undrained
1 large onion, sliced
1 bottle (14 ounces) ketchup
½ cup water
4 or 5 potatoes, peeled and cut in wedges (optional)

In a shallow bowl, mix flour, salt, and paprika. Dip both sides of steak pieces in mixture. Brown steak in a skillet in hot oil.

In a large bowl, mix together green pepper, mushrooms, onion, ketchup, and water. Place alternating layers of steak and vegetables in a slow cooker. Cook on low heat about 8 hours. If desired, add potato wedges to the slow cooker for the last 3 hours.

Serves 8 to 10

Family Tip: Have picnics. Eating together in a more casual setting is a lot of fun and creates memories, whether it's at the beach, in the canyon, in the back-yard, or in the family room by the fireplace during winter.

SPICY ORANGE BEEF

There's a world of difference here between home-cooked and take-out.

2	tablespoons cornstarch
1	cup beef broth
¼	cup soy sauce
¼	cup orange juice
¼	cup orange marmalade
½	teaspoon (or less) crushed red pepper flakes
2	tablespoons olive oil
1	pound sirloin or New York steak, cut diagonally in thin strips
3 to 4	tablespoons grated orange peel
1	clove garlic, minced
½	teaspoon ground ginger
4	cups hot cooked rice

In a medium bowl, combine cornstarch, broth, soy sauce, orange juice, marmalade, and red pepper flakes. Set aside.

In a large skillet or wok, heat oil over medium-high heat. Add half of steak strips and stir-fry for 3 minutes, until browned and nearly cooked through. Remove first half to a plate; cook second half of strips. Return all strips to skillet or wok. Add orange peel, garlic, and ginger; stir-fry 1 minute.

Pour cornstarch mixture over steak strips, stirring constantly. Bring to a boil over medium heat, cooking until sauce thickens. Serve over rice.

Serves 4

Chicken

Vary these enchiladas by using cooked ground beef or shredded pork.

1	cup chopped onion
1	clove garlic, minced
2	tablespoons butter or olive oil
1	can (14½ ounces) tomatoes
1	can (8 ounces) tomato sauce
1	teaspoon sugar
1	teaspoon cumin
½	teaspoon salt
½	teaspoon oregano
½	teaspoon basil
½ to 1	can (4 ounces) diced green chiles
8 to 10	flour tortillas
2	cups cooked, cubed chicken — see p. 55
2	cups grated cheddar, Monterey Jack, or Mexican blend cheese
½	cup sour cream

Heat oven to 350° F. Grease a 9- x 13-inch baking dish or spray with nonstick cooking spray.

In a large skillet, sauté onion and garlic in butter or olive oil. Add tomatoes, tomato sauce, sugar, cumin, salt, oregano, basil, and green chiles. Bring to a boil; reduce heat and simmer, covered, for 20 to 25 minutes.

In the center of each tortilla, spoon some chicken, 2 tablespoons sauce, and 2 tablespoons cheese. Roll and place seam side down in baking dish. Mix together sour cream and remaining sauce. Spread over tortillas. Top with remaining cheese. Cover with foil. Bake for 30 minutes.

Serves 8 to 10

HAWAIIAN BARBECUE CHICKEN

Host a Hawaiian Luau for your family dinner and serve this chicken as the main course.

4 to 6   boneless, skinless chicken breasts
   1   cup barbecue sauce
   1   can (20 ounces) crushed pineapple, undrained
   1   teaspoon ground ginger
   1   tablespoon cornstarch

Heat oven to 350° F.

Place chicken breasts in a baking dish that has been greased or sprayed with nonstick cooking spray. In a shallow bowl, stir together barbecue sauce, pineapple, ginger, and cornstarch. Pour over chicken. Cover with aluminum foil and bake for 1 to 1½ hours.

Serves 4 to 6

APRICOT CHICKEN

One of the quickest dishes that you can make.

4 to 6   boneless, skinless chicken breasts
   1   envelope dry onion soup mix
   1   jar (10 ounces) apricot or orange marmalade

Heat oven to 350° F.

Place chicken breasts in a 3-quart casserole or 9- x 13-inch baking dish that has been sprayed with nonstick cooking spray. Mix dry onion soup and marmalade in a small bowl and spread over chicken. Bake, uncovered, for 30 to 40 minutes.

Serves 4 to 6

CHICKEN ENCHILADAS WITH AVOCADO SALSA

Nearly everyone will enjoy these enchiladas with avocado salsa.

FOR ENCHILADAS:

1	medium onion, chopped
1	tablespoon butter or olive oil
1	can (10¾ ounces) cream of chicken soup
2	cups sour cream
2	cups Mexican blend, cheddar, or Monterey Jack cheese
3 to 4	boneless, skinless chicken breasts, cooked and diced — *Pc 55*
½	teaspoon chili powder
1	can (4 ounces) diced green chiles
1	can (2¼ ounces) sliced black olives
8 to 10	flour tortillas

FOR AVOCADO SALSA:

3 to 4	avocados, diced
2 to 3	tomatoes, diced
2	tablespoons minced cilantro
	Juice of 1 lime
¼	teaspoon chili powder (more, if desired)
½	teaspoon salt
¼	teaspoon pepper

In a small skillet, sauté onion in butter or olive oil until soft. In a large bowl, combine sautéed onion, soup, sour cream, and cheese. Put half of sauce in another bowl and set aside. In the first bowl, add chicken, chili powder, green chiles, and olives; mix well.

Heat oven to 350° F. Fill the center of each tortilla with chicken mixture. Roll and place seam down in a greased 9- x 13-inch pan. Spread the reserved sauce on top. Cover and bake for 25 to 30 minutes. Uncover and bake an additional 10 minutes. Serve with Avocado Salsa.

To make salsa, combine all ingredients in a medium bowl.

Serves 4 to 5 (two tortillas per person)

SOUTHWEST CHICKEN ROLLS

Here's a southwestern approach to the popular Chicken Dumplings.

FOR CHICKEN ROLLS:

2 boneless, skinless chicken breasts, cooked and diced — p. 55
¼ green pepper, chopped
¼ red pepper, chopped
2 tablespoons chopped green onions
½ cup frozen or canned corn
¼ cup black beans, rinsed and drained
1 tablespoon minced fresh parsley
½ cup chopped spinach
1 tablespoon olive oil
¼ teaspoon salt
¼ teaspoon pepper
1 teaspoon cumin (less, if desired)
1 tablespoon minced jalapeño pepper or canned diced green chiles
1 teaspoon chili powder (less, if desired)
⅛ teaspoon cayenne pepper
2 cans (8 ounces each) crescent rolls

FOR CUCUMBER RANCH DRESSING:

1 medium cucumber, peeled
½ cup mayonnaise
¼ cup sour cream
½ cup buttermilk
2 green onions, chopped
3 tablespoons minced fresh parsley
Pinch salt
Pinch pepper
Pinch cayenne pepper
⅛ teaspoon onion powder
1 teaspoon celery seed
⅛ teaspoon garlic powder
¼ teaspoon paprika

124

Heat oven to 350° F.

In a large bowl, mix chicken, green pepper, red pepper, green onions, corn, black beans, parsley, spinach, olive oil, salt, pepper, cumin, jalapeño pepper or green chiles, chili powder, and cayenne pepper.

Separate crescent rolls and place a spoonful of chicken mixture in the center of each roll. (Or press the edges of two rolls together for a larger roll and fill with two spoonfuls of chicken mixture.) Fold corners toward middle and seal.

Place rolls on a baking sheet that has been greased or sprayed with non-stick cooking spray. Bake for 15 to 20 minutes, until rolls are light brown. Serve with Cucumber Ranch Dressing spooned over the top.

To make Cucumber Ranch Dressing, puree cucumber in a food processor. Add mayonnaise, sour cream, buttermilk, green onions, parsley, salt, pepper, cayenne pepper, onion powder, celery seed, garlic powder, and paprika. Blend until well mixed. Refrigerate for several hours before serving. Makes about 2½ cups dressing.

This dressing is also great on green salads.

Serves 6 to 8

Save Money: Can or freeze fresh produce from your garden or from a produce market. This will be less expensive than buying canned vegetables. It's also healthier for your family since canned goods have a lot of preservatives.

HONEY-GLAZED CHICKEN

Try it both ways—with or without curry.

3	tablespoons butter or margarine, melted
¼	cup prepared mustard
½	cup honey
1	teaspoon salt
1	teaspoon curry powder (optional)
4 to 6	boneless, skinless chicken breasts

Heat oven to 350° F.

In a shallow bowl, mix melted butter, mustard, honey, salt, and curry, if desired. Roll chicken pieces in mustard mixture. Place in a 7- x 11-inch or 9- x 13-inch baking dish. Bake, uncovered, for 40 to 50 minutes, basting occasionally. Allow chicken to stand 5 minutes after it is done so the glaze can thicken.

Serves 4 to 6

Family Tip: If your children are grown or older, turn dinnertime into a forum for discussion of current issues and events in the area and around the world. It beats the doldrums of the evening news but serves to keep everyone informed. Keep your conversations lively but friendly.

RANCH CHICKEN

Putting popular Ranch Dressing on chicken is another way to enjoy it.

⅔	cup crushed cornflakes
⅔	cup grated Parmesan cheese
1	envelope ranch dressing mix
6 to 8	boneless, skinless chicken breasts
½	cup butter or margarine, melted

Heat oven to 350° F.

Mix cornflakes, cheese, and dressing mix in a shallow bowl. Dip chicken breasts in butter; then roll in ranch dressing mixture. Place chicken in a 9- x 13-inch pan. Bake, uncovered, for 45 minutes.

Serves 6 to 8

SWEET-AND-SOUR CHICKEN

Always a hit and easy to prepare.

1	clove garlic, minced
¼	cup chopped onion
2	tablespoons olive oil
4	boneless, skinless chicken breasts, cut into 1-inch pieces
½	cup + 1 to 2 tablespoons water
1	teaspoon chicken bouillon granules
1	can (20 ounces) pineapple chunks, drained and juice reserved
½	green pepper, sliced
1	large tomato, cut in wedges
½	cup cider vinegar
½	cup sugar
1	tablespoon soy sauce
½	teaspoon salt
2	tablespoons cornstarch
4 to 6	cups hot cooked rice

In a large skillet, sauté garlic and onion in olive oil. Add chicken and cook until cooked through and lightly browned. Add ½ cup water and bouillon and bring to a boil. Add pineapple, green pepper, and tomato.

In a small bowl, mix reserved pineapple juice, vinegar, sugar, soy sauce, and salt. Add to chicken mixture; bring to a boil. In a small bowl, stir together cornstarch and water until smooth. Add to pan and cook until sauce is thickened. Serve with rice.

Serves 4 to 6

Family Tip: Make Sunday dinner special by serving it in the dining room with a pretty tablecloth and your best dishes and silverware.

SESAME CHICKEN

Family members of all ages will like this simple, yet flavorful chicken.

4 to 6	boneless, skinless chicken breasts
	Approximately 1 cup soy sauce
1	cup flour
½	cup sesame seeds
2	tablespoons olive oil

Place chicken breasts in a glass pan or resealable plastic bag. Add enough soy sauce to cover chicken, about 1 cup. Marinate in refrigerator for about 30 minutes.

Heat oven to 325° F.

In a shallow bowl, mix together flour and sesame seeds. Dredge chicken pieces in flour mixture. Heat oil in a large skillet (ovenproof if available) and brown chicken on both sides. Put chicken in a baking dish or keep in ovenproof skillet and bake for 20 minutes, uncovered.

Serves 4 to 6

Family Tip: During dinner, ask family members to say something they appreciate about the person sitting next to them.

CHICKEN WITH PINEAPPLE-STRAWBERRY SALSA

The Pineapple-Strawberry Salsa also makes a great accompaniment to fish, such as salmon, halibut, swordfish, or sole.

FOR CHICKEN:

1	tablespoon olive oil
½	teaspoon salt
¼	teaspoon pepper
1	clove garlic, minced
3 to 4	boneless, skinless chicken breasts
2	tablespoons butter

FOR SALSA:

1	cup diced fresh pineapple
½	cup diced strawberries
1	kiwifruit, peeled and diced
¼	cup chopped red onion or green onions
1	jalapeño pepper, seeded and chopped
1	teaspoon cornstarch
¼	cup orange juice

In a small bowl, mix oil, salt, pepper, and garlic. Brush both sides of each chicken breast with mixture. In a large skillet, cook chicken in melted butter until lightly browned and cooked through, about 8 to 10 minutes. Remove from skillet to a platter; keep warm.

To make salsa, in a medium bowl, combine pineapple, strawberries, kiwifruit, onion, and jalapeño. Set aside.

In a small bowl, mix cornstarch and orange juice until well blended. Put in skillet in which chicken was cooked and cook until slightly thickened. Pour over salsa. Arrange chicken on platter; spoon salsa over chicken.

Serves 4

"FRIED" CHICKEN

*Crusty oven-fried chicken can be made at home, and then refrig-
erated for a picnic later.*

6 to 8	boneless, skinless chicken breasts
1	teaspoon salt
¼	teaspoon pepper
1	egg, slightly beaten
2	tablespoons milk
½	cup flour
⅔	cup Parmesan cheese
1	cup dry bread crumbs
1	teaspoon paprika
2 to 3	tablespoons butter or margarine, melted

Heat oven to 350° F.

Season chicken with salt and pepper. Mix egg and milk in a shallow
bowl. Mix flour, Parmesan cheese, bread crumbs, and paprika in another
shallow dish. Dip chicken breasts in egg mixture and then in flour mixture. Place chicken in a 9- x 13-inch baking pan or on a 12- x 17-inch
baking sheet that has been sprayed with nonstick cooking spray.
Drizzle with melted butter. Bake 30 to 40 minutes, uncovered. Serve hot
or chilled.

Serves 6 to 8

*Save Money: Save stale bread by placing it in a
brown paper bag. Use for bread puddings and stuffing or put it in a food processor or blender to make
dry bread crumbs.*

131

THAI PEANUT CHICKEN

Rice sweetened with coconut milk is the perfect companion to this spicy chicken.

FOR CHICKEN:

3 to 4	boneless, skinless chicken breasts
¾	cup medium or hot salsa
¼	cup peanut butter (creamy or chunky)
2	tablespoons lime juice
1	tablespoon soy sauce
1	teaspoon grated fresh gingerroot

FOR RICE:

1½ to 2	cups rice
1	can (14 ounces) coconut milk
1½ to 2	cans coconut milk cans of water (adjust to amount of rice)

FOR SERVING:

2 to 3	tablespoons minced cilantro
½	cup chopped peanuts

Place chicken breasts in a slow cooker. In a small bowl, mix salsa, peanut butter, lime juice, soy sauce, and gingerroot. Pour mixture over chicken. Cook on high until hot; then turn to low. Cook for 5 to 6 hours. Before serving, remove chicken from cooker and pull apart into large pieces. Return to sauce and stir.

Make the rice allowing sufficient time for it to cook before the chicken in done. Put rice, coconut milk, and water in a rice cooker or large saucepan. Cook until rice is done, about 20 to 25 minutes.

Put cilantro and peanuts in separate small bowls to be sprinkled on individual servings of chicken mixture over rice.

Serves 4 to 6

ROASTED CHICKEN

Sometimes forgotten, roasted whole chickens are extremely easy to prepare and offer the perfect taste of "home cooking."

1	whole chicken (2½ to 3 pounds)
1	medium onion
2	tablespoons butter, melted or olive oil
2	cloves garlic, minced
1	teaspoon basil
1	teaspoon salt
½	teaspoon ground sage
½	teaspoon thyme
½	teaspoon lemon pepper

Heat oven to 375° F.

Rinse chicken and pat dry. Put whole onion in cavity. Place chicken, breast side up, on a rack in a roasting pan. Brush with butter or olive oil. Rub skin of chicken with garlic.

In a small bowl, mix together, basil, salt, sage, thyme, and lemon pepper. Rub chicken with seasonings.

Roast, uncovered, for 1 to 1¼ hours until chicken is cooked through or a meat thermometer registers 180° to 185° F.

Remove from oven, cover with foil to keep warm, and let rest for 10 minutes to retain juices before carving.

Serves 4 to 6

FAR EAST CHICKEN

Bacon-wrapped chicken with a Far Eastern flair.

½	cup soy sauce
¼	cup sugar
1	teaspoon salt
1	teaspoon ginger
1	teaspoon paprika
4 to 6	boneless, skinless chicken breasts
2 to 3	slices bacon, cut in halves

Heat oven to 350° F.

Mix soy sauce, sugar, salt, ginger, and paprika in a large baking dish or resealable plastic bag. Marinate chicken in sauce for several hours in refrigerator. Wrap each chicken breast with a half slice of bacon; secure with toothpick. Bake, uncovered, for 30 to 40 minutes.

Serves 4 to 6

Save Time: Buy boneless, skinless chicken breasts so you do not have to debone and skin them. Buy chicken tenders if needing small pieces of chicken.

This is homecooked comfort food at its best.

2 to 3	chicken breasts
3	cups water
1 to 2	tablespoons curry powder
	Dash salt and pepper
1	package (6 ounces) Uncle Ben's Long Grain and Wild Rice
2	tablespoons butter
1	cup sliced mushrooms
2	celery stalks, sliced
½	small onion, chopped
1	can (10¾ ounces) cream of chicken soup
1	cup sour cream

Heat oven to 400° F.

In a large saucepan, cook chicken in water with curry, salt, and pepper. Remove chicken, reserving liquid. Cut chicken into bite-size pieces. Cook rice in seasoned water (about 2½ cups). Melt butter in a large skillet and sauté mushrooms, celery, and onion.

In a large bowl, mix chicken pieces, rice, mushroom mixture, soup, and sour cream. Pour into a greased or sprayed 3-quart baking dish. Bake for 30 minutes, or until thoroughly heated.

Serves 6

Save Money: Buy chicken breasts with bones in and remove them yourself. It's not a difficult or very time-consuming process and much less expensive than buying boneless, skinless breasts.

135

CHICKEN STROGANOFF

A new version of traditional stroganoff.

2 to 3	boneless, skinless chicken breasts, cut in 2-inch strips
1½	cups sliced mushrooms
½	cup chopped onion
½	cup chopped green or red pepper
3	tablespoons butter
3	tablespoons flour
1	cup chicken broth
¼	cup sour cream
½	teaspoon salt
¼	teaspoon pepper
¼	teaspoon nutmeg
	Cooked wide noodles or other pasta

In a large skillet, sauté chicken, mushrooms, onion, and green or red pepper in butter until chicken is no longer pink and vegetables are soft. In a small bowl, mix flour and chicken broth, stirring until smooth. Pour into skillet. Bring mixture to a boil, reduce heat, and cook until thickened. Add sour cream, salt, pepper, and nutmeg. Heat through but do not allow to boil. Serve over hot noodles.

Serves 4

CHICKEN DIJON

Dijon mustard adds class to any meat dish.

4	boneless, skinless chicken breasts
2	tablespoons butter
1	clove garlic, minced
3	tablespoons minced onion
1	cup sliced mushrooms
3 to 4	tablespoons Dijon mustard
1	cup half-and-half
3 to 4	cups hot cooked rice

In a large skillet, cook chicken in melted butter over medium heat until cooked through. Remove from skillet. Sauté garlic, onion, and mushrooms in pan drippings, adding more butter if needed. Stir in mustard and half-and-half. Cook on low heat, stirring until sauce is slightly thickened. Return chicken to pan, turning to coat in sauce. Simmer until chicken is heated through, being careful not to let sauce boil. Serve over rice.

Serves 4

Save Time: Make double amounts of recipes; then store the additional portion in the refrigerator or freezer to reheat for a quick meal.

ORIENTAL CHICKEN BUNDLES

Camp cooking never tasted so good.

4	squares (16 inches each) of heavy-duty aluminum foil
12	tablespoons uncooked instant rice
4	boneless, skinless chicken breasts
1	cup sliced carrots
1	large onion, sliced, separated into rings
1	green pepper, julienned or sliced
1	red pepper, julienned or sliced
¼	cup water
¼	cup Worcestershire sauce
¼	cup soy sauce
4	tablespoons butter

Heat oven to 350° F.

In the center of a square of foil, place 3 tablespoons rice. Add chicken breast, and one-fourth of the carrots, onion, green pepper, and red pepper. Repeat for remaining 3 pieces of foil.

In a small bowl, combine water, Worcestershire sauce, and soy sauce. Pour equal amounts over each chicken and vegetable bundle. Dot each with 1 tablespoon butter. Secure foil by bringing sides up and folding over several times. Fold over the ends. Place bundles on a baking sheet and bake for 1 hour, or longer, until chicken is cooked through. Open foil carefully to let steam escape.

Serves 4

Cooking Tip: You can cook these bundles in the coals of a campfire too.

CHICKEN WITH CHERRY SAUCE

Cherries aren't just for pie filling!

½	cup milk
1	cup flour
1	teaspoon thyme
½	teaspoon salt
¼	teaspoon pepper
4 to 6	boneless, skinless chicken breasts
1½	tablespoons olive oil
1	can (16 ounces) unsweetened pie cherries, drained and juice reserved
¼	cup brown sugar
¼	cup sugar
1	teaspoon prepared mustard
1	tablespoon cornstarch dissolved in a little water
2 to 3	drops red food coloring

Heat oven to 350° F.

Put milk in a shallow bowl. Put flour, thyme, salt, and pepper in another shallow bowl, stirring to mix. Dip chicken first in milk and then in flour mixture. In a large skillet, brown chicken on each side in olive oil. Transfer to a 3-quart baking dish. Cover with foil and bake for 25 minutes.

Meanwhile, put ½ cup reserved cherry juice in a medium saucepan. Add cherries, brown sugar, sugar, and mustard; mix well. Add cornstarch dissolved in a little water. Stir in food coloring. Bring to a boil; reduce heat and cook until slightly thickened, about 5 minutes.

After baking chicken for 25 minutes, remove foil and pour prepared cherry sauce over top. Continue baking, uncovered, for 15 more minutes.

Serves 4 to 6

HONEY-MUSTARD CHICKEN

This recipe is a great dish when entertaining dinner guests.

FOR HONEY-MUSTARD SAUCE:

⅓	cup Dijon mustard
⅓	cup honey
1½	teaspoons olive oil
1	teaspoon lemon juice

FOR CHICKEN:

1	tablespoon olive oil
4	chicken breasts
	Salt and pepper to taste
1½	cups sliced mushrooms
2	tablespoons butter
4	slices bacon, cut in halves and cooked
½	cup grated Monterey Jack cheese
½	cup grated cheddar cheese

In a small bowl, stir together mustard, honey, oil, and lemon juice. Put chicken breasts in a glass dish or resealable plastic bag. Add ⅔ of Honey Mustard Sauce. Marinate in refrigerator for about 2 hours.

Heat oven to 375° F.

In a large skillet, heat olive oil. Discard marinade and cook marinated chicken breasts until browned on the outside and no longer pink in the center, sprinkling with salt and pepper during cooking. Place cooked chicken in a 7- x 11-inch or 9-inch square baking dish that has been greased or sprayed with nonstick cooking spray. Baste with remaining Honey Mustard Sauce.

Sauté mushrooms in butter. Put 2 half pieces of bacon and some sautéed mushrooms on each chicken breast. Sprinkle cheeses on top.

Bake for 10 to 12 minutes.

Serves 4

Pork

BARBECUED PORK CHOPS

Slow baking with barbecue sauce tenderizes these pork chops.

4 to 6	pork chops
1	tablespoon olive oil
½	cup ketchup
1	cup water
1	teaspoon salt
1	teaspoon celery seed
½	teaspoon nutmeg
1	bay leaf
4 to 6	cups hot cooked rice

Heat oven to at 325° F.

Brown pork chops in olive oil in a large skillet. Mix ketchup, water, salt, celery seed, nutmeg, and bay leaf in a small bowl. Place pork chops in a 7- x 11-inch or 9- x 13-inch baking dish or 3-quart casserole. Cover with sauce. Bake, covered, for 1½ hours. Remove bay leaf before serving. Serve over rice.

Serves 4 to 6

Family Tip: Make cooking dinner part of your family vacation plans. When traveling, rent a place with a kitchen so you can cook part of the time. Trips to local food markets can be an adventure in themselves.

PORK CHOPS WITH GRAVY

These pork chops make their own delicious gravy while baking.

6   pork chops
1   tablespoon olive oil
1   can (10¾ ounces) cream of chicken soup
3   tablespoons ketchup
2   teaspoons Worcestershire sauce
    Hot mashed potatoes, noodles, or rice

Heat oven to 350° F. In a large skillet, brown pork chops on both sides in olive oil. In a medium bowl, combine soup, ketchup, and Worcestershire sauce, mixing well. Place pork chops in a 7- x 11-inch, 9- x 13-inch, or 3-quart baking dish that has been greased or sprayed with nonstick cooking spray. Cover chops with sauce. Bake, covered, for 1 hour. Serve gravy over potatoes, noodles, or rice.

Serves 6

PORK AND BEANS

A new definition of pork 'n' beans.

4   pork chops
1   teaspoon salt
½   teaspoon pepper
1   tablespoon olive oil
1   can (31 ounces) pork and beans
4   thick onion slices
4   green pepper slices

Heat oven to 350° F. Sprinkle pork chops with salt and pepper, then brown both sides in olive oil in a large skillet. Spread beans in a 3-quart baking dish and then lay pork chops on beans. Top with onion and green pepper slices. Bake, covered, for 1 hour.

Serves 4

MONTEREY PORK CHOPS

Perky pork chops.

4 to 6	pork chops
1	tablespoon olive oil
1	can (15 ounces) tomato sauce
1	can (4 ounces) diced green chiles
1	cup grated Monterey Jack cheese
4 to 6	cups hot cooked rice

In a large covered skillet, brown pork chops in olive oil. Pour tomato sauce and chiles over pork chops. Bring to a boil; then reduce heat and cook, covered, on low heat for 45 minutes. Sprinkle cheese over pork chops and cook another 5 minutes, or until cheese is melted. Serve over rice.

Serves 4 to 6

PORK CHOPS WITH ONIONS

Just the right blend of flavors.

4	pork chops
2	teaspoons seasoning salt
1	teaspoon black pepper
1	tablespoon olive oil
1	large onion, sliced
1	cup water

Rub both sides of pork chops with seasoning salt and pepper. In a large skillet, heat oil, then brown pork chops on both sides. Add onion and water. Cover and simmer for 20 to 25 minutes. Spoon onions over pork chops to serve.

Serves 4

STUFFED PORK CHOPS

Ask the butcher to cut a pocket in extra-thick pork chops for you.

4 to 6	pork chops (1 inch thick each)
1	tablespoon olive oil
1¼	cups bread crumbs or stuffing mix
½	teaspoon salt
¼	teaspoon pepper
1	tablespoon minced fresh parsley
½	teaspoon sage or poultry seasoning
2 to 3	tablespoons chopped onion
1	cup finely diced apples
1	cup milk

Heat oven to 350° F.

Cut a pocket in each pork chop or have your butcher do this for you.
Lightly brown both sides of pork chops in a skillet in olive oil. Let
cool slightly.

In a medium bowl, combine bread crumbs or stuffing mix, salt, pepper,
parsley, sage or poultry seasoning, onion, apples, and milk; mix well.
With a spoon, stuff each pork chop with stuffing mixture; close with
toothpicks, if necessary.

Place pork chops in a shallow baking dish that has been greased or
sprayed with nonstick cooking spray. Cover with lid or foil. Bake for 40
to 45 minutes.

Serves 4 to 6

146

*Save Money: Make your own bread crumbs in a
food processor or blender by using stale bread. You
can also use fresh bread and then toast the crumbs.*

CREAMY PORK CHOP CASSEROLE

Gives "casserole" a good name.

4 to 6	pork chops (preferably boneless)
1	tablespoon olive oil
1½	cups uncooked rice
1	can (10¾ ounces) cream of celery soup
1	can (10¾ ounces) chicken rice soup
¾	cup milk
1	medium onion, sliced
1	small green pepper, sliced
2	carrots, sliced

Heat oven to 350° F. Brown pork chops on both sides in a large skillet in olive oil.

Mix rice, cream of celery soup, chicken rice soup, and milk in a medium bowl. Transfer soup mixture to a shallow 3-quart baking dish. Place pork chops on top of mixture. Put onion, green pepper, and carrot slices on top of pork chops. Cover and bake for 1 hour, or until rice is tender.

Serves 4 to 6

Family Tip: Just for fun, have a "backwards" dinner. Start with dessert, then have the main course, and then the salad.

PORK ROAST WITH ROSEMARY

Fresh herbs really make a big difference in flavor.

1	boneless pork roast (3 to 4 pounds)
½	cup chopped onion
2½	cups chicken broth, divided
¼	cup red wine vinegar
2	tablespoons olive oil
3	cloves garlic, minced
1	tablespoon minced fresh or 1 teaspoon dried rosemary
1	teaspoon salt
½	teaspoon pepper
2	tablespoons cornstarch
⅓	cup cold water

Put roast in a glass baking dish or a large resealable plastic bag. In a small bowl, combine onion, ½ cup broth, vinegar, olive oil, garlic, rosemary, salt, and pepper. Pour mixture over roast. Cover roast and marinate in refrigerator 4 to 6 hours, turning occasionally.

Heat oven to 350° F. Place roast in a roasting pan. Add remaining 2 cups chicken broth to marinade and pour over roast. Bake, uncovered, for 2 to 2½ hours, or until a meat thermometer registers 160° F to 170° F.

Place roast on a serving platter; let rest for 10 minutes before slicing in order for meat to retain juices. Skim off grease from pan juices. Mix cornstarch with water and add to juices. Bring to a boil, stirring until thickened. Serve gravy with roast.

Serves 6 to 8

Save Time: If several recipes you are preparing during the week call for chopped onion, green pepper, or cooked and diced chicken, prepare enough for all the meals at one time. Keep in containers or resealable bags in the refrigerator or freezer.

CRANBERRY PORK ROAST

Every kitchen should have a slow cooker so that dinner can be started early in the day. A tasty and nutritious meal will be then ready when the family gathers in the evening.

1	boneless pork roast (3 to 4 pounds), cut in half
2	tablespoons olive oil
1	can (16 ounces) cranberry sauce (not jelly)
½	cup sugar
¾	cup cranberry juice
1	teaspoon dry mustard
½	teaspoon salt
1	teaspoon pepper
½	teaspoon ground cloves
¼	cup cornstarch
¼	cup water

In a large skillet, brown roast in olive oil on all sides. Transfer to a slow cooker.

Combine cranberry sauce, sugar, cranberry juice, mustard, salt, pepper, and cloves in a small bowl. Pour over roast. Cover and cook on low heat for 6 to 8 hours or on high heat for 3 to 4 hours. Remove roast from slow cooker and place on platter.

In a saucepan, combine cornstarch and water, stirring until smooth. Add juice and cranberries from slow cooker. Bring to a boil and cook until sauce is thickened. Slice roast and serve cranberry sauce over the top.

Serves 8 to 10

ROAST PORK WITH PEACH SAUCE

This sweet and tangy peach sauce adds flair to slow-cooked pork.

1   boneless pork roast (3 to 4 pounds)
4   cups sliced fresh or canned peaches
⅔   cup ketchup
⅔   cup red wine vinegar
¼   cup soy sauce
¾   cup brown sugar
2   cloves garlic, minced
2   tablespoons grated fresh ginger

Place roast in a slow cooker. Cook on low for 5 to 6 hours. Remove from slow cooker and discard pan juices. Return to slow cooker.

Put peaches, ketchup, vinegar, soy sauce, brown sugar, garlic, and ginger in a food processor or blender. Process until well blended. Pour over roast and cook an additional 1 to 2 hours on low.

Serves 6 to 8

Save Time: Use bottled minced garlic rather than mincing your own.

This easy cherry sauce makes pork roast an elegant Sunday dinner.

1	teaspoon salt
1	teaspoon pepper
1	teaspoon sage
1	boneless pork loin roast (3 to 4 pounds)
1	can (16 ounces) pie cherries in water
1½	cups sugar
¼	cup vinegar
1	teaspoon cinnamon
1	teaspoon ground cloves
1	tablespoon lemon juice
3	tablespoons cornstarch
2 to 3	drops red food coloring

Heat oven to 325° F.

Combine salt, pepper, and sage in a small bowl. Rub roast with seasonings. Place roast in a roasting or baking pan. Bake, uncovered, for 2 to 2½ hours.

Fifteen minutes before roast is done, drain cherries, reserving juice. Add enough water to cherry juice to measure ¾ cup. Put ½ cup of this juice in saucepan with sugar, vinegar, cinnamon, cloves, and lemon juice. Bring to a boil. Mix cornstarch with remaining ¼ cup cherry juice. Add to saucepan. Cook until thickened. Add cherries and food coloring. Remove roast from oven and slice. Serve with cherry sauce.

Serves 8 to 10

APPLE STRUDEL PORK TENDERLOIN

They always say apples and pork go together—and they surely do here.

1	pork tenderloin (2 to 3 pounds)
	Salt and pepper to taste
1½	tablespoons olive oil
1	package (21 ounces) frozen apple strudel pastry
1 to 2	teaspoons cinnamon

Heat oven to 400° F.

Sprinkle tenderloin with salt and pepper. In a large skillet or roasting pan, sear tenderloin in olive oil, browning on all sides.

Unfold apple strudel and lay tenderloin in the middle, spreading apples evenly on pastry. Sprinkle with cinnamon. Fold pastry together and seal. Place in a baking pan. Bake for 40 minutes.

Serves 6 to 8

Family Tip: As a family, volunteer at a local soup kitchen or food bank. This will help family members appreciate dinner at home even more and gain satisfaction in serving others.

Pork tenderloin is a tender cut of meat but best served with a sauce for flavor.

2	envelopes brown gravy mix
1⅓	cups water
½	cup soy sauce
⅓	cup red wine vinegar
2	cloves garlic, minced
2	pork tenderloins (2 pounds each), cut into ½-inch slices
2 to 3	tablespoons olive oil
2 to 2½	cups fresh mushrooms, sliced
1	large onion, sliced
	Hot mashed potatoes or cooked rice

In a medium bowl, whisk together gravy mix, water, soy sauce, vinegar, and garlic.

In a large skillet, brown both sides of tenderloin slices in hot olive oil. Add gravy mixture, mushrooms, and onion. After bringing to a boil, reduce heat, cover, and cook for 10 to 15 minutes. Serve over mashed potatoes or rice.

Serves 8 to 10

SWEET-AND-SOUR SPARERIBS

Buying meaty, boneless spareribs with little fat makes for easier eating and is actually more economical.

4 to 5	pounds spareribs
½	cup brown sugar
½	cup sugar
2	tablespoons cornstarch
1	cup ketchup
⅔	cup vinegar
½	cup water

Heat oven to 350° F.

Place ribs on a rack in a shallow roasting pan. Bake, uncovered, for 1½ hours. While ribs are baking, combine sugars and cornstarch in a medium saucepan. Stir in ketchup, vinegar, and water. Bring to a boil. Cook, stirring constantly, until mixture is thickened and clear.

Remove ribs from roasting pan. Discard drippings. Remove rack and return to ribs to pan. Cover with sauce. Bake 30 more minutes.

Serves 6

PORK NOODLES

A real transformation of those packaged noodles!

1	tablespoon olive oil
1	pork tenderloin (about ¾ pound), cut in ¼-inch strips
2	packages (3 ounces each) pork-flavored ramen noodles
1½	cups water
1	medium red pepper, thinly sliced
1	cup broccoli florets
4 to 5	green onions, cut in 1-inch pieces
1	tablespoon minced parsley
1½	tablespoons soy sauce

Heat olive oil in a large skillet or wok over medium heat. Add pork; stir-fry about 5 minutes, until pork is no longer pink. Break apart noodles and add to pork. Add seasoning packets, water, red pepper, broccoli, green onions, parsley, and soy sauce. Bring mixture to a boil, cooking 3 to 5 minutes and stirring occasionally, until noodles are tender.

Serves 4

PULLED PORK SANDWICHES

*Pulled pork sandwiches are always popular and will be a
favorite in your kitchen too.*

4 to 5   pounds pork shoulder or loin roast
1   bay leaf
1   teaspoon crushed red pepper flakes (more or less, if desired)
4   cups water
1   cup cider vinegar
⅓   cup brown sugar
3   tablespoons ketchup
1   tablespoon Worcestershire sauce
1   teaspoon dry mustard
1   clove garlic, minced
1   teaspoon salt
6   large sandwich buns or rolls

Trim fat from pork. Put pork, bay leaf, red pepper flakes, and water in a
large soup pot or Dutch oven. Bring to a boil. Reduce heat and simmer,
covered, for 4 to 5 hours until pork is tender. Put pot in refrigerator to
cool pork in broth. When cool, remove pork and shred with two forks.

Put 3 cups of the cooking liquid into a large saucepan and add vinegar,
brown sugar, ketchup, Worcestershire sauce, mustard, garlic, and salt.
Bring to a boil; reduce heat and cook for about 10 minutes, until sugar is
dissolved and flavors blend. Add shredded pork and heat through. Serve
on sandwich buns or crusty rolls.

Serves 6

Fish

A spectacular but simple way to present halibut. To make this dish low-fat, use low-fat cheese and light butter.

1	pound halibut fillets or steaks
1	cup grated cheddar cheese
¼	cup butter
½	cup chopped onion
⅓	cup chopped green bell pepper
⅓	cup chopped red bell pepper
2	tablespoons flour
1	teaspoon salt
½	teaspoon pepper or white pepper
1	cup milk
2	tablespoons butter, melted
½	cup seasoned bread crumbs

Wrap halibut in foil and steam for 20 minutes in a covered pan with 1 to 2 inches water. Break cooked halibut into chunks and place in a 9- x 13-inch baking dish. Sprinkle with grated cheese.

In a medium saucepan, melt ¼ cup butter, and then sauté onion and peppers until soft. Stir in flour, salt, and pepper. Gradually add milk. Stir continuously until mixture is thick and bubbly. Pour sauce over fish and cheese.

In a bowl, stir 2 tablespoons melted butter into bread crumbs. Sprinkle bread crumbs on top of sauce.

Bake at 400° F for 20 minutes.

Serves 6

HALIBUT WITH BASIL SAUCE

Cook other fish—such as salmon, cod, or sole—with this scrumptious sauce.

⅓ cup flour
1   teaspoon paprika
1   teaspoon salt
⅛ teaspoon pepper
4   halibut fillets or steaks
1   small onion, chopped
¼ cup butter or margarine
1   cup sour cream
1   teaspoon basil

In a large resealable plastic bag, combine flour, paprika, salt, and pepper. Add halibut and shake, coating each piece.

In a large skillet, sauté onion in butter until soft. Remove from pan and set aside. Place halibut in skillet and cook over medium heat about 6 to 8 minutes on each side, or until fish flakes easily. Place halibut on a platter. Return onions to skillet and add sour cream and basil. Heat through, but do not boil. Serve sauce over halibut.

Serves 4

Save Time: Type your basic shopping list on the computer. Keep a copy in the kitchen to add to during the week. Add specialty items for particular recipes.

Have your fish cake and eat it, too!

2	tablespoons olive oil, divided
1	pound white fish (cod, halibut, or sole)
1	egg, beaten
¼	cup thinly sliced green onions
2½	tablespoons mayonnaise
1	tablespoon fresh lemon juice
2	tablespoons Dijon mustard
¾	cup bread crumbs
2 to 3	tablespoons minced fresh parsley
2 to 3	drops Tabasco sauce (more, if desired)
¼	teaspoon salt
¼	teaspoon freshly ground pepper
	Tartar sauce
	Lemon wedges

Heat oven to 400° F.

Place 1 tablespoon olive oil in a baking dish. Add fish, turning once to coat with oil. Bake 15 to 20 minutes, until fish flakes easily. Let cool, pat dry with paper towels, and flake with a fork.

In a large bowl, combine fish, egg, green onions, mayonnaise, lemon juice, mustard, bread crumbs, parsley, Tabasco sauce, salt, and pepper. Stir gently until mixture holds together.

Form mixture into 8 patties. Heat 1 tablespoon olive oil in a large skillet. Cook fish cakes on medium heat until brown on each side and cooked through. Serve with tartar sauce and lemon wedges.

Serves 4

Family Tip: Begin early as newlyweds to have family dinners together.

SURF AND TURF

You'll think you're at the finest restaurant in town when you eat this Surf and Turf.

1	tablespoon butter
1	pound New York steak, cut in thin strips
1½	pounds frozen jumbo shrimp, thawed
½	pound sugar peas
¼	teaspoon salt
¼	teaspoon pepper
1	pint grape tomatoes or halved cherry tomatoes
1	teaspoon minced garlic
3	tablespoons minced fresh parsley
1½	teaspoons grated lemon peel
1	tablespoon lemon juice
4 to 6	slices Texas toast, buttered
	Lemon wedges

Melt butter in a large skillet. Add steak, then shrimp, peas, salt, and pepper. Cook over medium-high heat, stirring often until shrimp and steak are nearly cooked. Add tomatoes and garlic to skillet. Cover, and shaking pan several times, cook 2 more minutes until tomatoes soften. Stir in parsley, lemon peel, and lemon juice.

Broil toast 2 to 3 minutes in oven or toaster, turning once, until golden. Butter one side.

Serve steak and shrimp mixture with toast and lemon wedges.

Serves 4 to 6

Cooking Tip: Heat lemons or oranges in microwave for 1 minute before squeezing. They will yield more juice.

SHRIMP FAJITAS WITH TOMATO SALSA

Make the marinade and salsa ahead of time. Buy ready-to-cook shrimp. Then dinner will be done in just a few minutes.

FOR SHRIMP:

3	green onions, thinly sliced
3	tablespoons fresh lime juice
1	teaspoon grated lime peel
1	teaspoon olive oil
1	clove garlic, minced
½	teaspoon cumin
½	teaspoon coriander
½	teaspoon chili powder
¼	teaspoon salt
¼	teaspoon red pepper flakes
1	pound medium shrimp, peeled and deveined
1	tablespoon olive oil

FOR TOMATO SALSA AND SERVING:

3	medium tomatoes, diced
½	cup sliced radishes
½	cup chopped red onion
1	jalapeño pepper, seeded and minced
1 to 2	tablespoons minced cilantro
8	tortillas, warmed
	Sour cream
1 to 2	avocados, diced

In a large bowl, combine onion, lime juice, lime peel, 1 teaspoon olive oil, garlic, cumin, coriander, chili powder, salt, and red pepper flakes. Add shrimp, stirring to coat. Marinate for 5 to 10 minutes.

Remove shrimp from marinade. In a large skillet, heat 1 tablespoon olive oil and cook shrimp for about 3 to 4 minutes, until pink.

In a medium bowl, combine tomatoes, radishes, onion, jalapeño pepper, and cilantro to make salsa.

Serve shrimp in tortillas with Tomato Salsa, sour cream, and avocados.

Serves 4

SHRIMP AND PASTA

Buy the best Parmesan cheese you can find; it's worth the money.

1	package (12 ounces) bowtie or penne pasta, cooked according to package directions and drained
2 to 3	cloves garlic, minced
2 to 3	tablespoons olive oil
2	cups mushrooms, sliced
2	tablespoons minced fresh basil
1	teaspoon salt
½	teaspoon pepper
8	Roma tomatoes, chopped
1	pound shrimp, deveined and tails removed
4	green onions, chopped
2	tablespoons minced fresh cilantro or parsley
¼	cup freshly grated Parmesan cheese

While pasta is cooking, sauté garlic in olive oil in a large skillet. Add mushrooms, basil, salt, and pepper, cooking until mushrooms are tender. Stir in tomatoes and shrimp, and cook until shrimp turns pink. Add green onions and cilantro or parsley. Sprinkle with Parmesan cheese. Serve over pasta.

Serves 6

Save Time: Dovetail preparation steps by cutting or chopping one item while another is simmering or baking.

BAKED SALMON WITH DILL SAUCE

Fantastic fast fish!

4 to 6   salmon fillets
Lemon pepper
Litehouse Dill Vegetable Dip

Preheat oven to 425° F.

Place salmon in a baking pan that has been buttered or sprayed with nonstick cooking spray. Sprinkle with lemon pepper. Bake 15 to 20 minutes, until fish flakes easily in center.

Remove pan from oven and spread a thin layer of vegetable dip over salmon. Return pan to oven and broil for a few minutes until dip lightly browns.

Serves 4 to 6

Family Tip: Have family members take turns cooking dinner. Adults can assist younger children in planning and preparing meals.

SALMON WITH PAPAYA-MANGO-PINEAPPLE SALSA

Your family just may want more salsa than salmon when they have this dish—it's so good. For variety, try making this recipe using halibut.

1	mango, diced
1	papaya, diced
1	cup fresh pineapple, diced
3	green onions, chopped
3	tablespoons fresh lemon juice
3 to 4	tablespoons minced cilantro
2	tablespoons jalapeño pepper, seeded and chopped or 2 tablespoons diced green chiles (more if desired)
1	teaspoon salt
4 to 6	salmon fillets

In a medium bowl, combine mango, papaya, pineapple, onions, lemon juice, cilantro, and jalapeño pepper or chiles. Mix well; set aside.

Put 1½ inches of water in skillet, add salt, and bring to a boil. Reduce heat so that water boils gently. Add salmon and cover skillet. Cook for about 8 to 10 minutes, until salmon flakes easily in the middle. (Or brush salmon with extra-virgin olive oil and cook on grill, grilling 5 to 6 minutes per side until done.) Serve with salsa.

Serves 4 to 6

Family Tip: Turn dinnertime into a cultural experience by preparing ethnic dishes and talking about the particular country or culture from which the food comes. Try eating the way people of that culture do: for example, use chopsticks for Japanese cuisine or eat with your fork in your left hand when eating a European meal.

GINGER SALMON

Salmon is a healthy choice as it is rich in protein, vitamins A and the B-group, and omega-3 oils.

⅓	cup brown sugar
2	tablespoons honey
2	tablespoons butter
2	tablespoons Dijon mustard
2	tablespoons soy sauce
2	tablespoons olive oil
2 to 3	teaspoons freshly grated ginger
4 to 6	salmon fillets
	Salt and pepper
1	onion, sliced
1 to 2	lemons, sliced

Heat oven to 375° F.

In a small saucepan, mix brown sugar, honey, butter, mustard, soy sauce, and olive oil. Heat until sugar is dissolved. Add ginger.

Place salmon fillets in a baking dish that has been greased or sprayed with nonstick cooking spray. Sprinkle lightly with salt and pepper. Place onion and lemon slices on salmon, then pour sauce over. Cover with foil and bake for about 20 minutes, until center of salmon flakes easily.

Makes 4 to 6 servings

Save Time: Use nonstick cooking spray to grease skillets and baking pans.

CAJUN SALMON

When the kids want Mac 'n' Cheese, fix this for the adults.

　　　　　Cajun spices (Blackened Seasoning, Creole Seasoning or
　　　　　Emeril's Bayou Blast)
2 to 4　　salmon fillets

Sprinkle desired amount of Cajun spices on top of fillets. Turn over and sprinkle on other side. Wrap in plastic wrap and place in a glass baking dish. Microwave on high for 8 to 10 minutes, or until fish flakes easily. Check during cooking time. Or bake, covered, at 425° F for 15 to 20 minutes.

Serves 2 to 4

SALSA FISH

Talapia, relatively new to many markets, is a versatile, mild, and inexpensive fish.

　　　　　Olive oil
4 to 6　　talapia fillets (orange roughy, cod, sole, red snapper, or halibut
　　　　　may be substituted)
1　　　　jar (12 or 16 ounces) salsa
½ to 1　　cup grated mozzarella cheese

Heat olive oil in a medium or large skillet. Sear fillets on one side; turn and sear on other side. Pour salsa over fish. Cover and cook 7 to 10 minutes, until fish flakes easily. Top with cheese and cook covered 1 to 2 minutes more until cheese is melted.

Serves 4 to 6

Cooking Tip: If cooking a large piece of salmon, score down the middle with a knife to facilitate even cooking.

SALMON WITH VEGETABLES

Just add a green salad and you will have a filling and healthy meal for your family.

4 to 6	large squares aluminum foil
4 to 6	salmon fillets
4 to 6	onion slices, one per fillet
1 to 2	potatoes, thinly sliced
2 to 3	carrots, thinly sliced
	Salt and pepper

Heat oven to 450° F.

On a large square of aluminum foil, place a salmon fillet, an onion slice, 4 to 5 slices of potato, and a handful of carrot slices. Sprinkle with salt and pepper. Fold and seal foil. Repeat for the number of servings you are making. Bake for 20 minutes.

Serves 4 to 6

Save Money: Generally, fish fillets cost more per pound than steaks. Cut your own fillets from halibut and salmon steaks with a sharp, thin-bladed knife. A fillet is simply fish without bone and is cut from boned steaks.

FILLET OF SOLE WITH GRUYERE CHEESE

Any mild, white fish can be used in this excellent recipe. Buy extra on sale and freeze for another night.

3 tablespoons butter
1 large onion, sliced
2 cups mushrooms, sliced
1 cup grated Gruyere cheese
4 fillets sole
   Salt and freshly ground pepper to taste
¾ teaspoon paprika
4 sprigs fresh parsley (optional)

Heat oven to 400° F.

Melt butter in a heavy skillet and lightly sauté onion and mushrooms until soft, about 5 minutes. Butter a shallow baking dish and cover the bottom of the dish with half of the onion and mushroom mixture. Sprinkle with half of the cheese. Place fillets in baking dish. Top fillets with remaining onions and mushrooms, then remaining cheese. Season with salt, pepper, and paprika.

Bake for 20 minutes, then brown quickly under the broiler until the cheese bubbles. Garnish with sprigs of parsley if desired.

Serves 4

MEDITERRANEAN FISH

Choose any fish you like—halibut, sole, cod, snapper, or orange roughy.

- 6   tablespoons feta cheese
- 6   tablespoons diced tomato
- 6   tablespoons sliced black olives
- 6   teaspoons minced fresh basil (more if desired)
- 6   tablespoons chopped marinated artichoke hearts, reserve marinade
- 6   fish fillets
- 6   large squares heavy-duty aluminum foil

Heat oven to 450° F.

In a small bowl, combine cheese, tomato, olives, basil, and artichoke hearts, adding a little marinade from the artichokes. Place 1 fillet of fish in the center of a square of heavy-duty aluminum foil. Spoon 3 to 4 tablespoons of cheese mixture over fish. Secure foil by bringing sides up and folding over several times. Fold over the ends. Repeat for remaining 5 fillets. Place packets on a baking sheet and bake for 15 minutes, or until fish flakes easily with a fork.

Makes 6 servings

Family Tip: Go camping together. When staying on a seacoast or near a lake or river, you can even catch your own fish for dinner!

PARMESAN ORANGE ROUGHY

Terrific with herbed rice and steamed vegetables.

3   tablespoons butter
2   tablespoons flour
1   teaspoon salt
½   teaspoon pepper
¾   cup grated Parmesan cheese
1   egg, beaten
4   orange roughy fillets
     Lemon wedges

Heat oven to 450° F.

Melt butter in a 2-quart or 9-inch square baking dish.

Combine flour, salt, pepper, and cheese on a plate. Beat egg in a shallow
dish. Dip fillets in egg, then coat in flour-cheese mixture. Place fillets in
prepared baking dish and bake 2 minutes. Turn fillets over and continue
cooking 10 to 13 minutes longer, until fish flakes easily and turns white.
Serve with lemon wedges.

Serves 4

SOUR CREAM TUNA CASSEROLE

A sophisticated interpretation of tuna casserole.

3	cups egg noodles, cooked *al dente* and drained
2	cans (6 ounces each) albacore tuna fish in water, drained
½	cup diced celery
⅓	cup chopped green onions
¾	cup sour cream
1	teaspoon prepared mustard
½	cup mayonnaise
½	teaspoon thyme
¼	teaspoon salt
1	small zucchini, thinly sliced
1	cup grated Monterey Jack or cheddar cheese
1	tomato, diced

Heat oven to 350° F. Spray a 2- or 3-quart casserole dish with nonstick cooking spray.

In a large bowl, combine cooked noodles, tuna fish, celery, green onions, sour cream, mustard, mayonnaise, thyme, and salt. Spread half of mixture in casserole dish. Place a layer of zucchini over noodles. Top with remaining noodle mixture, followed by remaining zucchini. Sprinkle cheese over top. Bake for 30 minutes. Five minutes before casserole is finished baking, sprinkle tomatoes on top.

Serves 6

Family Tip: Hold a "crazy hat dinner." Invite each family member to wear his or her favorite or funniest hat to the table.

COCONUT SHRIMP

These shrimp are baked, not fried.

FOR SHRIMP:

1	cup flaked coconut
½	cup plain bread crumbs
½	teaspoon salt
	Dash cayenne pepper
1½ to 2	pounds shelled and deveined medium to large shrimp
¼	cup honey

FOR SAUCE:

1	jar (12 ounces) cocktail sauce
1	tablespoon grated fresh gingerroot

Heat oven to 425° F.

Line a large baking sheet with foil. Spray foil with cooking spray.

To make the shrimp, put coconut, bread crumbs, salt, and cayenne pepper in a food processor. Process for 10 seconds to lightly mix. Pour mixture into a shallow bowl or pie plate.

Pat shrimp dry with paper towels and put in a medium bowl. Heat honey in microwave or in a saucepan over low heat until liquid. Pour over shrimp, stirring to coat.

Roll several shrimp at a time in coconut mixture to coat. Place on baking sheet. Bake for 10 to 12 minutes, until lightly browned.

To make the sauce, combine cocktail sauce and gingerroot in a small bowl. Serve with shrimp.

Serves 4 to 6

Pasta, Rice, and Eggs

MACARONI AND CHEESE

Macaroni and cheese—the essence of comfort food! It's a flexible dish. Just add onion, mustard, cream cheese, sour cream, cottage cheese, or bread crumbs.

2	tablespoons butter or margarine
2	tablespoons flour
½	teaspoon salt
¼	teaspoon pepper or white pepper
2	cups milk
2 to 3	cups grated medium or sharp cheddar cheese
1	package (8 ounces) elbow macaroni, cooked according to package directions and drained

OPTIONAL INGREDIENTS

¼ to ½	cup chopped onion
1	teaspoon dry mustard or 1 to 2 teaspoons Dijon mustard
1	package (8 ounces) cream cheese
½	cup sour cream
½	cup cottage cheese
⅓	cup fine bread crumbs, mixed with 2 tablespoons melted butter or margarine

Melt butter in a large saucepan. (Sauté onion, if using.) Stir in flour, salt, and pepper and cook 1 minute. (Add mustard, if using.) Add milk; cook and stir over medium heat until slightly thickened. Add cheese, stirring until melted. (Add either cream cheese, sour cream, or cottage cheese, if using.) Stir in cooked macaroni.

Serve immediately or transfer to a 2-quart baking dish. (Sprinkle with bread crumbs, if using.) Bake, uncovered, at 350° F for 25 to 30 minutes.

Serves 4 to 6

Save Money: Low-fat cottage cheese can be substituted for more expensive ricotta cheese. Freeze cottage cheese, then thaw and drain well.

THREE-CHEESE JUMBO SHELLS

Meatless and magnificent. If you're short on time, substitute 3 to 4 cups spaghetti sauce from a jar for the homemade sauce here.

FOR SAUCE:

¼	cup chopped onion
1	clove garlic, minced
1	tablespoon olive oil
1	can (14½ ounces) diced tomatoes, undrained
1	can (8 ounces) tomato sauce
1	teaspoon sugar
1	teaspoon oregano
¼	teaspoon thyme
1	bay leaf

FOR SHELLS:

10	jumbo shells or manicotti shells, cooked according to package directions
2	eggs, beaten
1	cup grated mozzarella cheese
1	cup ricotta cheese
½	cup grated fresh Parmesan cheese
¼	cup chopped fresh parsley
½	teaspoon oregano
¼	teaspoon pepper (more if desired)

Heat oven to 350° F.

To make sauce, sauté onion and garlic in hot oil in a 2- or 3-quart saucepan. Add tomatoes, tomato sauce, sugar, oregano, thyme, and bay leaf. Boil, then reduce heat and simmer, uncovered, for 20 minutes. Remove from heat; discard bay leaf.

After cooking shells, drain and rinse in cold water. In a medium bowl, combine eggs; mozzarella, ricotta, and Parmesan cheeses; parsley, oregano, and pepper. Spoon cheese mixture into shells.

Pour ½ cup of sauce into a 2- or 3-quart baking dish. Place shells in dish. Pour remaining sauce over shells. Cover with foil or lid of baking dish. Bake for 40 minutes, or until heated through.

Serves 5 to 6

SIMPLE LASAGNA

The liquid in this recipe softens the lasagna noodles while baking so they don't need to be precooked.

½	pound Italian sausage
1	jar (32 ounces) spaghetti sauce
¾	cup water
1	package (8 ounces) lasagna noodles
1	container (15 ounces) ricotta cheese
12	ounces mozzarella cheese, grated or sliced
¼	cup Parmesan cheese, grated

Heat oven to 375° F.

Brown sausage in a large skillet. Drain grease. Add spaghetti sauce and water; simmer. In a 9- x 13-inch baking pan put a layer of sauce, then uncooked lasagna noodles, then ricotta cheese, then mozzarella cheese. Repeat layers, ending with sauce. Sprinkle with Parmesan cheese. Cover with foil and bake for 1 hour. Remove foil. Let stand 10 minutes before cutting.

Serves 8 to 10

SPAGHETTI PIE

Your family will request this often.

- 6 ounces spaghetti, cooked according to package directions and drained
- 2 tablespoons butter
- ⅓ cup Parmesan cheese
- 2 eggs, beaten
- 1 pound ground beef
- ½ cup chopped onion
- ¼ cup chopped green pepper
  Salt and pepper
- 1 can (8 ounces) tomato sauce or 1 can diced tomatoes (more if desired)
- 1 can (6 ounces) tomato paste
- 1 tablespoon sugar
- 2 teaspoons Italian seasoning or 1 teaspoon oregano and 1 teaspoon basil
- ½ teaspoon garlic salt
- 1 cup ricotta cheese
- ½ cup grated mozzarella cheese

Heat oven to 350° F.

Return cooked and drained spaghetti to cooking pot. Put butter on hot spaghetti. Add Parmesan cheese and eggs. Mix well. Transfer to a 10-inch pie plate or 7- x 11-inch baking dish.

In a large skillet, brown ground beef with onion and green pepper, lightly seasoning with salt and pepper. Drain grease. Add tomato sauce or tomatoes, tomato paste, sugar, oregano, and garlic salt. Simmer for 10 minutes.

Spread ricotta cheese on spaghetti crust. Pour tomato mixture over cheese. Bake, uncovered, for 20 minutes. Sprinkle mozzarella cheese on top. Bake 5 minutes longer, until cheese melts.

Serves 6

GARDEN SPAGHETTI

Use the bounties of your garden or a farmers market in this creamy spaghetti sauce.

2	cups broccoli florets
1½	cups sliced zucchini
1½	cups sliced mushrooms
1	large carrot, sliced
1	tablespoon olive oil or butter
¼	cup chopped onion
2	cloves garlic, minced
2	tablespoons butter
2	tablespoons flour
2	teaspoons chicken bouillon granules
1	teaspoon thyme
2	cups milk
½	cup grated Swiss cheese
½	cup grated mozzarella cheese
8	ounces spaghetti, cooked according to package directions and drained
	Grated Parmesan cheese

In a large skillet, sauté broccoli, zucchini, mushrooms, and carrots in olive oil until crisp-tender.

In a large saucepan, sauté onion and garlic in butter until soft. Stir in flour, bouillon, and thyme until well blended and cook for 1 to 2 minutes until thickened. Gradually add milk. Bring to a boil, reduce heat, and cook until thickened. Add Swiss cheese and mozzarella cheese, stirring until cheeses are melted. Add vegetables and heat through.

Serve vegetable sauce over spaghetti. Sprinkle with Parmesan cheese.

Serves 4

FETTUCCINI

Such an accommodating dish! Serve it as a side dish, or top with cooked chicken or steamed vegetables as a main dish.

- 1   package (8 ounces) cream cheese
- ¾   cup grated Parmesan cheese + more for serving
- ½   cup butter or margarine
- ½   cup milk
- 8   ounces fettuccini, cooked according to package directions and drained

In a large saucepan, combine cream cheese, ¾ cup Parmesan cheese, butter, and milk. Cook on low heat, stirring until smooth, about 10 minutes. Place cooked fettuccini in a bowl and add sauce, stirring to evenly distribute sauce over pasta. Sprinkle with additional Parmesan cheese.

Serves 4 to 6

Save Money: Buy items you use frequently in quantities; this makes the cost per unit less.

Rivals any restaurant pasta.

2	cups broccoli florets
1	tablespoon olive oil
1	cup cubed cooked ham
2	cloves garlic, minced
3	tablespoons flour
2½	cups milk
	Coarse salt to taste
	Freshly ground black pepper to taste
1	package (3 ounces) cream cheese
8 to 10	ounces linguini (spinach or plain, cooked according to package directions)
¼	cup grated fresh Parmesan cheese + more for serving

Cook broccoli in boiling water in a large saucepan about 5 minutes, until crisp-tender. Drain and set aside.

In a saucepan, heat olive oil and cook ham until lightly browned. Add garlic and sauté about 1 minute. Add flour; stir while cooking 1 to 2 minutes. Gradually add milk, stirring constantly, and cook until mixture thickens, about 5 minutes. Add salt and pepper. Add cream cheese, stirring until melted.

Combine linguini, broccoli, ham mixture, and ¼ cup Parmesan cheese, heating through. Sprinkle with additional Parmesan cheese, if desired.

Serves 4 to 6

Family Tip: Begin dinnertime discussion with the question, "What was the best thing about your day?" Dinner table conversation will be positive, enlightening, and perhaps hilarious.

CHICKEN AND MUSHROOM PASTA

Keep a wide variety of pastas in your pantry so you can be ready for many different meals, including this one. This dish also works well with penne pasta or fettuccini.

1	package (8 ounces) bowtie pasta, cooked according to package directions and drained
2 to 3	boneless, skinless chicken breasts, cut in bite-size pieces
	Salt and freshly ground pepper to taste
2	tablespoons butter
½	cup chopped onion
1	clove garlic, minced
1 to 1½	cups button or crimini mushrooms, halved
1 to 2	tablespoons flour
⅓	cup white grape juice or apple juice
½	cup half-and-half or cream
2 to 3	tablespoons minced fresh parsley (optional)

Put drained pasta back in cooking pot and set aside. Sprinkle chicken pieces liberally with salt and pepper. In a large skillet, melt 1 tablespoon butter over medium-high heat. Sauté onion and garlic until soft, about 2 to 3 minutes. Add chicken and cook about 5 to 6 minutes. Remove to a bowl or plate. Add remaining 1 tablespoon butter to skillet. Put mushrooms in skillet. Season lightly with salt and pepper. Sauté about 5 minutes, until tender. Mix flour and grape juice or apple juice in a small bowl or cup, stirring until smooth. Add to mushrooms. Cook, stirring constantly, about 2 to 3 minutes.

Turn heat to low. Add half-and-half or cream, stirring until mixture thickens slightly. Add chicken mixture to pasta. Stir in parsley, if desired.

Serves 4

Family Tip: If getting your family members to the dinner table is a real challenge, use a little creativity: send each family member a personalized invitation to dinner.

PASTA WITH CREAMY PUMPKIN SAUCE

This is not your usual pasta sauce, but it's one you'll want to try.

1	cup grated Parmesan cheese + more for serving
1	package (8 ounces) cream cheese, cubed
¼	cup butter
½	cup milk
1	can (16 ounces) pumpkin
¼ to ½	teaspoon cayenne pepper
¼ to ½	teaspoon nutmeg
1	package (16 ounces) penne pasta, cooked according to package directions and drained

In a large saucepan, combine Parmesan cheese, cream cheese, butter, and milk. Cook over low heat, stirring frequently, until cream cheese is melted. Add pumpkin, cayenne pepper, and nutmeg, mixing well. Heat through, but do not boil. Add pasta, tossing lightly. Sprinkle with additional Parmesan cheese before serving.

Serves 6

Family Tip: Hold an international Christmas dinner and prepare foods from a different country each year. Try choosing a country from which your ancestors came. A German Christmas might include rouladen on the menu. A Scottish Christmas might include leek soup, salmon, and shortbread. For Brazil, serve feijoada and passion fruit mousse.

HERBED TOMATO PASTA

Grow your own herbs in a container on your patio or in your garden. Then you'll have the freshest herbs at very little cost.

12	ounces bowtie pasta, cooked according to package directions and drained
¼	cup butter
½	teaspoon beef bouillon granules
2	teaspoons minced fresh basil
1	teaspoon minced fresh rosemary
1	teaspoon minced fresh sage
2	cans (15 ounces each) diced tomatoes
1	teaspoon salt
¼	teaspoon pepper
¾	cup heavy cream

While pasta is cooking, melt butter in a large skillet. Add bouillon, basil, rosemary, and sage, stirring to blend. Add tomatoes and season with salt and pepper. Cook about 5 to 8 minutes. Add cream. Cook over medium heat, stirring frequently, until sauce is thickened. Serve over pasta.

Serves 4 to 6

Cooking Tip: A pastry blender can do more than cut butter into flour. Use it to chop canned tomatoes, hardboiled eggs, or avocados.

This is a good basic tomato sauce and can be used as a spring-board for many dishes.

1	tablespoon butter
2 to 3	tablespoons olive oil
½	cup chopped onion
2 to 3	cloves garlic, minced
3	tablespoons minced fresh parsley
1	can (14 ounces) diced tomatoes or 2 to 3 large tomatoes, diced
2	teaspoons dried basil or 2 tablespoons minced fresh basil
	Salt
	Pinch cayenne pepper or crushed red pepper flakes
¼ to ½	cup toasted pine nuts (optional)
4 to 6	ounces angel hair pasta, cooked according to package directions and drained
	Grated fresh Parmesan or Romano cheese

Put butter and olive oil in a saucepan. Sauté onion and garlic until soft. Add parsley, tomatoes, basil, salt, and cayenne pepper or red pepper flakes. Cook over medium heat until well blended and slightly thickened. Add pine nuts, if desired.

Serve over hot pasta. Sprinkle with Parmesan or Romano cheese.

Serves 2

PASTA WITH PESTO

Pesto is a traditional Italian mix of herbs and oils. This version features basil, garlic, pine nuts, and Parmesan cheese—a change of color and flavor from tomato sauces.

2	cups gently packed fresh basil
4	sprigs Italian parsley
2	cloves garlic, minced
1	teaspoon salt
¼	cup pine nuts
½ to ¾	cup olive oil
¾	cup grated Parmesan cheese
	Freshly ground pepper to taste
1	package (12 ounces) fettuccini, fusilli or other pasta, cooked according to package directions and drained
2	tomatoes, diced or 12 cherry tomatoes, halved

In a food processor, combine basil, parsley, garlic, salt, pine nuts, and olive oil. Blend until smooth and creamy, adding more olive oil if needed. Add Parmesan cheese and pepper to taste.

Put hot pasta and pesto in a large bowl and toss. Top with tomatoes.

Serves 4 to 6

Save Time: When making lasagna or manicotti, thin the sauce with a cup of V-8 juice or tomato juice. This eliminates the need to boil the pasta before layering the lasagna or filling the manicotti; the noodles will cook and soften during the baking process. You can also use no-cook lasagna noodles.

TOMATO-BASIL RISOTTO

Risotto—Italian rice—has a creamier texture than regular rice.

- 2 cans (14½ ounces) reduced-sodium chicken broth or 4 cups chicken broth
- 1 tablespoon butter
- 3 tablespoons chopped onion
- ½ teaspoon minced garlic
- 1½ cups diced tomatoes
- 1 cup Arborio rice
- 3 tablespoons minced fresh basil
- 3 tablespoons grated Parmesan cheese
- 1 tablespoon extra-virgin olive oil
- ⅛ teaspoon salt
- ⅛ teaspoon pepper

In a medium saucepan, bring broth to a boil. In a large saucepan, melt butter on medium heat and sauté onion and garlic until softened, about 2 minutes. Add tomatoes; cook 2 minutes. Add rice; cook 5 minutes, stirring constantly. Add ½ of broth and bring to a boil. Add remaining broth, ½ cup at a time, stirring and allowing rice to absorb liquid before adding more broth. When all the broth has been incorporated, add basil, Parmesan cheese, olive oil, salt, and pepper.

Serves 4

Family Tip: Use baby pictures of family members as place cards at the dinner table. During the meal, tell stories about each of the children and parents as babies and toddlers.

189

RICE PILAF

An excellent side dish to serve with fish, beef, ham, or chicken.

1   cup thinly sliced celery
½   cup chopped onion
1   small green pepper, diced
½   cup butter or margarine
1   cup long grain rice (not instant or quick-cooking)
2   chicken bouillon cubes or 2 teaspoons chicken bouillon granules
2½   cups boiling water
     Dash salt and pepper

Heat oven to 350° F.

In medium skillet, sauté celery, onion, and green pepper in butter for 5 minutes. Add rice and sauté 1 minute.

Dissolve bouillon cubes or granules in boiling water; add salt and pepper. Pour into a 2-quart baking dish. Add rice mixture. Cover and bake for 45 minutes. Uncover and stir. Bake 10 more minutes.

Serves 8

Save Time: Cook more rice than needed for a recipe and keep the rice (one week in the refrigerator and six months in the freezer) to use when preparing a quick dinner.

MEXICAN RICE

Muy bien! *Completes any Mexican dinner.*

2 teaspoons olive oil
½ teaspoon minced garlic
½ cup chopped onion
1 large tomato, chopped
1 cup rice
1 small green pepper, diced
Dash crushed red pepper flakes
½ teaspoon oregano
½ teaspoon salt
1 can (14 ounces) chicken broth

Heat oven to 400° F.

Heat oil in an ovenproof saucepan or Dutch oven over medium heat. Add garlic, onion, and tomato. Cook, uncovered, for 3 minutes, or until onion is soft. Add rice and cook 2 minutes, stirring until shiny and hot. Stir in green pepper, red pepper flakes, oregano, and salt. Add chicken broth. Bring to a boil, then bake, covered, for 15 to 20 minutes.

Serves 4 to 5

Family Tip: Jump-start your dinner table conversation by keeping a jar of conversation topics handy. Every now and then, pass the jar around the table and have family members draw a topic, such as, "What is your earliest memory?" "What was your favorite vacation and why?" or "What was your most embarrassing moment?"

ORZO WITH PINE NUTS

Orzo is a small pasta a little larger than long grain rice.

3 to 4	slices bacon
¾ to 1	cup sliced green onions
½	cup grated fresh Parmesan cheese, divided
1½	cups orzo, cooked and drained
½	cup pine nuts, toasted
1	teaspoon Italian seasoning
½ to 1	teaspoon seasoning salt

Cook bacon in a large skillet over medium heat, reserving drippings. Remove from pan and crumble. Add green onions to skillet and sauté about 2 minutes, until crisp-tender. Return bacon to pan; add ¼ cup Parmesan cheese, orzo, pine nuts, Italian seasoning, and seasoning salt. Cook 2 to 3 minutes, until heated through. Sprinkle with remaining ¼ cup Parmesan cheese.

Serves 6

SOUTHWEST RICE

Almost a meal in itself.

1	small green pepper, diced
1	small onion, chopped
1	tablespoon olive oil
1½	cups minute rice
1	cup salsa (mild, medium, or hot)
1½	cups chicken broth
1	cup frozen corn
1	cup grated cheddar or Mexican blend cheese

In a large skillet, sauté green pepper and onion in olive oil. Add rice, salsa, chicken broth, and corn. Bring to a boil; then reduce heat. Stir in cheese and cover skillet. Cook until rice is soft and cheese is melted.

Serves 6

GARLIC RICE

Lime and cilantro enhance this rice.

1	tablespoon olive oil
1 to 2	cloves garlic, thinly sliced
1	cup long grain rice, uncooked
2	cups water
2	tablespoons fresh lime juice
1	teaspoon salt
2	tablespoons minced cilantro
2	teaspoons grated lime peel

In a large saucepan, heat olive oil and sauté garlic for about 3 minutes, until light brown. Add rice and cook for 2 minutes. Add water, lime juice, and salt. Cook rice until liquid is absorbed, about 20 minutes. Mix in cilantro and lime peel.

Serves 2 to 4

COCONUT RICE WITH MANGO

Serve with halibut, salmon, or swordfish for a tropical treat. Small portions of this rich rice will satisfy.

1	cup jasmine rice, uncooked
2	cups light coconut milk
¾	cup milk
¾	cup sugar
1 to 2	mangoes, peeled and diced

Rinse rice several times with cold water. Place rice in a medium saucepan with coconut milk, milk, and sugar. Bring to a boil, cover, and cook on low heat about 25 minutes, until liquid is absorbed. Serve warm or at room temperature topped with diced mangoes.

Serves 2 to 4

BAKED OMELET

Occasionally, a lighter approach to dinner is welcomed. This is the perfect recipe for such a time.

½   cup flour
3   cups milk
8   eggs
1   teaspoon seasoning salt (or to taste)
3   cups grated cheddar cheese
¼   cup chopped onion
¼   cup chopped green pepper
¼   cup diced ham
¼   cup diced green chiles
¼   cup sliced pepperoni (optional)

Heat oven to 350° F.

Whisk flour, milk, and eggs together in a large bowl. Add seasoned salt and cheese. Add onion, green pepper, ham, chiles, and pepperoni, if desired. Pour mixture into a 9- x 13-inch baking pan that has been greased or sprayed with nonstick cooking spray.* Bake for 45 to 50 minutes, until eggs are set.

Serves 9 to 12

*Note: Recipe can be halved and baked in an 8- x 8-inch baking dish.

Save Time: Use your microwave to cook numerous foods, such as browning ground beef, cooking chicken breasts, heating casseroles, or scrambling eggs.

EGG BURRITOS

Also known as huevos rancheros.

FOR EGGS:

16 eggs
2 tablespoons milk
2 tablespoons chopped onion or green onions
1 can (4 ounces) green chiles, chopped (reserve 1 teaspoon)
1 to 2 tablespoons diced pimentos
¼ cup grated Monterey Jack cheese
Salt and pepper to taste
1 tablespoon butter (optional)
8 flour tortillas
Sour cream for serving (optional)
Salsa for serving (optional)

FOR TOMATO-AVOCADO SAUCE:

2 tomatoes, diced
2 avocados, diced
1 tablespoon chopped onion
1 teaspoon diced green chiles
1 tablespoon salsa
Minced garlic to taste

Thoroughly scramble eggs with milk; add onions, chiles, pimentos, cheese, and salt and pepper. Spray a large skillet with nonstick cooking spray or melt 1 tablespoon butter in skillet. Pour egg mixture in skillet and cook until eggs are done.

Place an inverted pie pan inside a large pan. Add water so that it fills the pan about 1 inch but does not touch the top of the pie pan. Place tortillas on top of pie pan, cover, and steam for 5 minutes to soften and heat them.

Fill burritos with eggs and top with Tomato-Avocado Sauce. Serve with sour cream and/or salsa, if desired.

To make Tomato-Avocado Sauce, combine tomato, avocado, onion, diced chiles, salsa, and garlic.

Serves 8

POTATO QUICHE

*Breakfast foods don't always have to be served in the morning.
Enjoy this for dinner along with fruit juice or fresh fruit.*

1	bag (24 ounces) frozen hash browns, thawed
⅓	cup butter, melted
1	cup grated Swiss or Monterey Jack cheese
1	cup grated cheddar cheese
1	cup diced ham, bacon, or cooked sausage
6	eggs
½	cup cream, half-and-half, or milk
½	teaspoon seasoning salt
	Dash nutmeg

Heat oven to 425° F.

Butter or spray a 9- x 13-inch baking dish with nonstick cooking spray.
Press a paper towel on thawed hash browns to remove excess moisture.
Spread hash browns in the bottom of the dish, forming a crust; press
them partway up sides of dish. Brush with melted butter. Bake for 25
minutes; then reduce heat to 350° F.

Remove dish from oven. Sprinkle cheeses and ham, bacon, or sausage
over top of crust. Beat eggs. Add cream, half-and-half, or milk; seasoning salt; and nutmeg. Pour over ham and cheeses. Bake for 20 minutes.

Serves 6 to 9

*Cooking Tip: Add a dash of salt to cream or eggs to
make them whip faster.*

WAFFLES

Who doesn't love a hot waffle? These light waffles don't take long to make and are superior to those that come from a box.

2	cups flour
1	tablespoon baking powder
1	teaspoon sugar
½	teaspoon salt
3	eggs, separated
1¾	cups milk
⅓	cup oil

In a large bowl, stir together flour, baking powder, sugar, and salt. Beat egg yolks and combine with milk and oil. Add to flour mixture and beat on medium until well mixed.

In a deep bowl, beat egg whites until stiff peaks form. Fold into flour mixture with a spatula.

Heat waffle iron. Pour about ½ cup batter onto grid, depending on size of waffle iron. Bake according to manufacturer's instructions.

Serve with warmed maple syrup, fruit syrup, fresh fruit, yogurt, sour cream mixed with brown sugar, or whipped cream.

Makes 6 to 8 waffles

Cooking Tip: Make sauce from leftover fruit juices by combining and cooking until thick: 1 tablespoon cornstarch, ¼ cup sugar, ¼ teaspoon cinnamon, and 1½ cups fruit juice. Serve sauce over fruit, pancakes, or waffles.

APPLE PANCAKES

An excellent weekend supper with perhaps bacon or sausage on the side.

7	tablespoons butter
2	large apples, peeled and sliced
6	eggs
3	tablespoons sugar
½	teaspoon salt
1½	cups milk
1	teaspoon vanilla
1	cup flour
½	teaspoon cinnamon
3	tablespoons brown sugar
	Maple syrup or jam

Heat oven to 400° F.

Put butter in a 9- x 13-inch glass baking pan; place in the oven until butter is melted, about 3 to 5 minutes. Remove pan from oven and arrange apple slices over melted butter. Return to oven and bake for 5 minutes to soften apples.

Put eggs, sugar, salt, milk, vanilla, flour, and cinnamon in a blender and blend until smooth. Pour batter over apples. Sprinkle with brown sugar. Bake for 20 minutes, until puffed and brown.

Serve with maple syrup or your favorite jam.

Serves 6

Vegetables

SEASONED ASPARAGUS

A little bit of seasoning peps up asparagus.

1   bunch asparagus, cut in 1-inch pieces
2   tablespoons butter
      Garlic salt to taste
      Pepper to taste

In a medium skillet, sauté asparagus pieces in butter. Sprinkle with garlic salt and pepper. Add a little water, cover, and cook until asparagus is crisp-tender.

Serves 4 to 6

ASPARAGUS IN ORANGE BUTTER

Grated orange peel and orange juice add great flavor to asparagus.

2   tablespoons butter, softened
1   tablespoon frozen orange juice concentrate, thawed
1   teaspoon grated orange peel
⅛   teaspoon onion powder
¼   teaspoon Dijon mustard
1   bunch fresh asparagus, trimmed
      Salt to taste

In a small bowl, combine butter, orange juice, orange peel, onion powder, and mustard. In a large skillet or saucepan, cook asparagus in a small amount of salted water, until tender, about 5 to 6 minutes. Drain asparagus and return to pan. Add butter mixture; cook until butter is melted and asparagus is coated.

Serves 4

ASPARAGUS WITH DILL SAUCE

This savory sauce can be used with most cooked vegetables to dress them up.

- 1   cup plain yogurt
- 2   tablespoons Dijon mustard
- ¼   cup mayonnaise
- 1   tablespoon fresh dill weed or 1 teaspoon dried dill weed
- 1   teaspoon thyme
- 2   bunches asparagus, trimmed

In a small bowl, combine yogurt, mustard, mayonnaise, dill weed, and thyme. Refrigerate for 30 minutes or more to blend flavors.

Cook asparagus in a vegetable steamer about 5 minutes, or until crisp-tender. Or cook in boiling water for 3 to 4 minutes. Plunge asparagus in cold water to stop cooking process, if desired. Place on a platter and pour sauce over top.

Serves 8

Save Time: Use quick cooking methods, such as steaming, microwaving, broiling, or stir-frying.

BLACK BEAN CASSEROLE

Tasty south-of-the-border fare.

2	cloves garlic, minced
1	medium onion, chopped
1½	tablespoons olive oil
2	cans (15 ounces each) black beans, rinsed and drained
½	cup tomato juice
2	tablespoons minced cilantro
1	can (4 ounces) diced green chiles (more, if desired)
1	teaspoon ground cumin
1	teaspoon salt

Heat oven to 375° F.

In a small skillet, sauté garlic and onion in olive oil. Transfer to a large bowl. Add black beans, tomato juice, cilantro, chiles, cumin, and salt. Stir. Place in a 9-inch square or 2-quart baking dish. Bake for 30 minutes.

Serves 6 to 8

Family Tip: Take time to occasionally read a story or article aloud to each other at the dinner table. You'll likely find that dinner is finished, but family members are lingering around the table to hear the end of the tale.

GREEN BEANS WITH CHEESE SAUCE

Green beans are good, but even better with this simple sauce.

1	package (10 ounces) frozen French-style green beans or haricot verts
2	tablespoons chopped onions
1 to 2	tablespoons butter
1	cup sour cream
⅓	cup (or more) cheddar cheese, grated

In a medium saucepan, cook beans according to package directions. Drain and set aside.

In a skillet, sauté onion in butter until tender. Add sour cream and cheese and cook on medium heat until cheese melts. Do not allow to boil.

Pour cheese sauce over beans and serve.

Serves 6

Save Time: Undiluted cream soups or cheese soups make easy sauces for vegetables or pasta.

COLORFUL GREEN BEANS

The colors as well as the flavors of green beans and red pepper complement each other.

2 to 2½ pounds fresh green beans, trimmed
2 to 3 tablespoons finely diced red onion
  1 small red bell pepper, seeded and coarsely chopped
  2 tablespoons butter
     Salt and pepper to taste

In a large saucepan, cook green beans in salted, boiling water about 12 to 15 minutes, until tender. Drain.

In a medium skillet, sauté onion and red pepper in butter, until softened. Add to beans and toss. Season with salt and pepper.

Serves 6 to 8

DILLED GREEN BEANS

Beans, which are easy to grow in a garden, yield during most of the season—giving you fresh beans for many summer dinners.

  1½ pounds fresh green beans, trimmed and cut in 3-inch pieces or 2 packages (10 ounces each) frozen French-cut green beans
  2 tablespoons butter
  1½ tablespoons fresh dill or ½ teaspoon dried dill
     Salt and freshly ground pepper to taste

Cook fresh green beans in a small amount of salted water for 15 minutes, or until tender. Drain. (Or place in a steamer and cook about 10 to 12 minutes.) Add butter, dill, and salt and pepper to taste.

Serves 6 to 8

GREEN BEANS IN SOUR CREAM

A happy blending of flavors.

1	pound of fresh green beans, trimmed
¼	cup chopped onion
2	cups mushrooms, sliced
2	tablespoons butter or olive oil
1	cup sour cream
1	teaspoon salt
½	teaspoon pepper
¼	teaspoon paprika

Cook beans in salted water about 10 to 12 minutes, until crisp-tender, or steam in a vegetable steamer for 10 minutes. Drain.

In a medium saucepan, sauté onion and mushrooms in butter or olive oil. Add sour cream, salt, pepper, and paprika. Simmer for 2 to 3 minutes, but do not let boil. Gently stir in beans.

Serves 6

Save Money: Plant a garden. Not only will growing your own vegetables and fruits save money, you cannot buy the taste of a just-picked tomato fresh from the garden.

LEMON BROCCOLI

Broccoli, rich in vitamin C, beta-carotene, and iron, is one of the best veggies you can eat for good health.

1 to ½	pounds fresh broccoli, cut into florets
¼	cup butter, melted
2½	tablespoons lemon juice
1	teaspoon lemon zest
1	cup sliced or slivered almonds

Steam broccoli in a vegetable steamer for 8 minutes or cook in a small amount of boiling water in a large saucepan for 8 to 10 minutes, until crisp-tender. Drain.

Melt butter in a small saucepan. Stir in lemon juice, zest, and almonds. Pour over broccoli.

Serves 4 to 6

SESAME BROCCOLI

Broccoli with an Asian flair.

1 to 1½	pounds fresh broccoli, cut in florets
1	tablespoon vinegar
4	teaspoons sugar
1	tablespoon olive oil
1	tablespoon soy sauce
1	tablespoon toasted sesame seeds

Steam broccoli in a vegetable steamer for 8 minutes or cook in a small amount of boiling water in a large saucepan for 8 to 10 minutes, until crisp-tender. Drain.

In a small saucepan, combine vinegar, sugar, oil, soy sauce, and sesame seeds. Heat, stirring until sugar dissolves and mixture is hot. Pour over broccoli.

Serves 4 to 6

BROCCOLI AND CAULIFLOWER IN CHEESE SAUCE

Two vegetables and a twist of orange in a mild cheese sauce.

2	cups cauliflower florets
2	cups broccoli florets
2	tablespoons butter
2	tablespoons flour
2	cups milk or half-and-half
1	tablespoon grated orange peel
½	teaspoon salt
⅛	teaspoon nutmeg
⅛	teaspoon pepper
½	cup grated cheddar cheese + extra for garnish

Put cauliflower and broccoli in a large saucepan with a small amount of salted water. Cook for 8 to 10 minutes, until crisp-tender. Drain. Place vegetables in an 8-inch square baking dish.

Heat oven to 325° F.

In a medium saucepan, melt butter. Add flour and stir until thickened, about 2 minutes. Gradually add milk or half-and-half, stirring until mixture thickens. Add orange peel, salt, nutmeg, pepper, and cheese. Cook until cheese melts. Pour sauce over vegetables. Sprinkle with additional grated cheese, if desired. Bake for 20 minutes.

Serves 4

APPLE CIDER CARROTS

Apple cider gives carrots a spark.

2   tablespoons butter
1   pound carrots (about 10), thinly sliced
¼   cup apple cider or apple juice
1   tablespoon brown sugar
2   teaspoons lemon juice
     Salt and pepper to taste

Melt butter in a large saucepan. Add carrots and cider. Cover and cook for 5 minutes, stirring occasionally. Add brown sugar and lemon juice. Season to taste with salt and pepper. Cook, uncovered, until liquid is almost absorbed and carrots are tender, stirring occasionally.

Serves 4 to 6

CARROTS AND MUSHROOMS

Remember how your mom told you that eating carrots would help you see better? Carrots are a rich source of beta-carotene, which actually does benefit your eyes.

4   cups sliced carrots
½   cup chopped green onions
1   cup sliced mushrooms
2 to 3 tablespoons butter
½   teaspoon ground ginger

In a medium saucepan, cook carrots in salted water until tender, about 8 to 10 minutes. Drain. Sauté green onions and mushrooms in butter. Add carrots and ginger. Simmer for 5 minutes.

Serves 8

BAKED CARROTS AND APPLES

Your family will want seconds of this delectable dish.

2½ to 3   cups sliced carrots
   2   large apples, peeled and thinly sliced
  ⅓   cup brown sugar
   2   tablespoons flour
  ½   teaspoon salt (or more)
  ¾   cup orange juice

Heat oven to 350° F.

In a medium saucepan, cook carrots in lightly salted water, about 5 to 8 minutes. Drain.

Place half the apples in a 2-quart baking dish that has been buttered or sprayed with nonstick cooking spray. Add half the carrots. Mix brown sugar, flour, and salt in a bowl. Sprinkle half of this over the carrots. Repeat a second layer of apples, then carrots, then brown sugar mixture. Pour orange juice over top. Bake for 20 to 25 minutes, until apples are tender.

Serves 4 to 6

Family Tip: During dinner, talk about memorable family vacations. You'll find that stressful incidents can even be laughable in retrospect—like the time Mom didn't have photo ID at the airport or the all-night, sleepless train ride from Florence to Bern.

CARROT SOUFFLÉ

You'll love this unusual presentation of carrots.

2	pounds carrots, peeled and cut into 1-inch pieces, or baby carrots
½	cup butter, softened
6	eggs
¾ to 1	cup sugar
6	tablespoons flour
2	teaspoons baking powder
2	teaspoons vanilla (less, if desired)

Heat oven to 350° F.

Boil carrots until tender; drain. Place butter, eggs, sugar, flour, baking powder, and vanilla in a food processor. Add carrots a little at a time. Blend until smooth. Pour into a 9- x 13-inch pan that has been greased or sprayed with nonstick cooking spray.* Bake for 50 minutes. Let stand 5 minutes before serving.

Serves 8 to 10

*Note: This recipe can be cut in half and prepared it in an 8- x 8-inch pan.

CHEESE AND CARROT SCALLOP

Carrots supreme.

10 to 12	large carrots, sliced
¼	cup butter
1	tablespoon dried onion flakes or ¼ cup chopped onion
¼	cup flour
2	cups milk
1	teaspoon salt
½	teaspoon dry mustard
¼	teaspoon celery salt
	Dash pepper
2 to 3	tablespoons butter
1	cup fresh bread crumbs
4 to 6	ounces Havarti or other cheese slices

In a medium saucepan, cook carrots in salted water for 8 to 10 minutes, until crisp-tender. Drain.

In another saucepan, melt ¼ cup butter. Add onion flakes or chopped onion and sauté until soft. Stir in flour until smooth. Add milk. Add salt, mustard, celery salt, and pepper. Cook, stirring constantly until thickened.

In a small saucepan, melt 2 to 3 tablespoons butter. Add bread crumbs and toss to coat.

Heat oven to 350° F.

Lightly grease or spray a 2-quart baking dish with nonstick cooking spray. Spread half the carrots, then half the cheese, in dish. Repeat layers. Pour sauce over all. Sprinkle with bread crumbs. Dot with remaining 1 tablespoon butter. Bake for 20 minutes, or until hot.

Serves 8

Family Tip: After children have left the nest, occasionally invite only one family at a time to dinner so that relationships can be nurtured in small numbers.

CHEESY CAULIFLOWER

Another time, try dill vegetable dip in place of mayonnaise and cheese in this recipe.

1	head cauliflower
½ to ¾	cup mayonnaise
½	cup grated high-quality Parmesan cheese

Heat oven to 375° F.

Trim cauliflower and separate into large florets. Wrap with plastic wrap, place in a glass dish, and add several tablespoons water. Microwave 2 to 3 minutes on high. Cauliflower should be crisp, but not raw. After it cools, dip individual florets in mayonnaise. Then twirl florets in Parmesan cheese, coating the tops. Return florets to baking dish, stem down. Bake for 8 to 10 minutes, until browned.

Serves 6

CREAMY CAULIFLOWER PUREE

Surprise your family with this vegetable and see if they can guess what it is.

1	head cauliflower, cut into florets
1 to 2	tablespoons butter
1	teaspoon salt
½	teaspoon pepper

Steam cauliflower or cook in salted water in a large saucepan until very tender. Drain. Put cauliflower, butter, salt, and pepper in a food processor. Blend until smooth. Adjust seasonings to taste.

Serves 6

BAKED CORN IN SOUR CREAM

Exceptional!

2	tablespoons butter
3	tablespoons diced onion
¼	cup finely diced celery
¼	cup flour
1	teaspoon salt
1	cup sour cream
1½	pounds frozen corn
6	slices bacon, cooked crisp and crumbled
1	tablespoon minced fresh parsley

Heat oven to 350° F.

In a large saucepan, melt butter. Sauté onion and celery until soft. Stir in flour and salt. Add sour cream gradually, stirring until mixture is smooth. Add corn, heating thoroughly. Stir in bacon and parsley. Pour into a 9- x 13-inch pan or 3-quart casserole dish that has been buttered or sprayed with nonstick cooking spray. Bake for 30 to 45 minutes.

Serves 8 to 10

Although you may be hesitant to spread mayo and cheese on corn, you'll be amazed at how delicious it is.

6	ears corn on the cob
¼	cup (approximately) mayonnaise (not Miracle Whip)
¼	cup (approximately) Parmesan cheese

Cook corn on the cob in boiling water for 6 minutes. (Or wrap in plastic wrap or wax paper and cook in the microwave for 12 to 14 minutes on high heat, rearranging once during cooking.) Spread a thin layer of mayonnaise on corn. Sprinkle with Parmesan cheese.

Serves 6

Note: Time is 2 to 4 minutes for 1 ear, 4 to 6 minutes for 2 ears, and 8 to 10 minutes for 4 ears. Times may vary depending on the microwave.

Family Tip: Every so often, listen to each other's music during dinner. Put a portable CD player in the kitchen and have each family member play a favorite song.

PEAS AND MUSHROOMS

You'll hear, "Pass the peas, please" with this dish.

- 1   small onion, chopped
- 6 to 8   medium or large mushrooms, sliced
- 1   tablespoon butter or margarine
- 1   bag (16 ounces) frozen peas
- 2   tablespoons water
- 1   tablespoon chopped pimiento (optional)

Sauté onion and mushrooms in butter in a medium skillet. Add peas and water. Heat through. Add pimiento. Be careful not to overcook.

Serves 6 to 8

CASHEW PEAS

An eye-catching vegetable dish—and tasty, too.

- 1   pound snow peas, ends trimmed
- 1   package (10 ounces) frozen peas
- 2 to 3   tablespoons butter
- ¼   teaspoon minced garlic
- 2   tablespoons chopped green onions
- 1   cup unsalted cashews or peanuts
- ½   teaspoon salt
- ¼   teaspoon freshly ground pepper
- 2   tablespoons minced fresh parsley

Cook snow peas in one pan and frozen peas in another pan, both in salted water until crisp-tender, about 3 to 5 minutes. Drain well and combine in one bowl.

In a small skillet, melt butter and sauté garlic, green onions, and cashews or peanuts, 1 to 2 minutes. Add salt, pepper, and parsley. Combine with peas and stir gently.

Serves 4 to 6

PEAS AND RED POTATOES

New red potatoes don't need to be peeled—one less step for a busy cook.

2   pounds red potatoes, quartered
1   bay leaf
¼   cup butter or margarine
1   teaspoon salt
⅛   teaspoon pepper
¼   teaspoon marjoram
¼   teaspoon thyme
1   package (10 ounces) frozen peas, thawed

Put potatoes and bay leaf in a large saucepan. Cover with water and bring to a boil. Cook about 15 to 20 minutes, until potatoes are tender. Drain; remove and discard bay leaf. Add butter, salt, pepper, marjoram, and thyme. Add peas and heat until cooked.

Serves 6

CREAM CHEESE POTATOES

There won't be any leftovers of these potatoes.

10 to 12   russet potatoes, peeled and quartered
       1   package (8 ounces) cream cheese
       1   cup sour cream
       2   teaspoons salt
       2   cloves garlic, minced
           Paprika
       1   tablespoon snipped fresh chives or minced parsley

Heat oven to 350° F.

In a large pan, boil potatoes in lightly salted water until soft. Drain. Put potatoes, cream cheese, sour cream, salt, and garlic in a large mixing bowl. Blend with an electric mixer until smooth (add milk, if needed).

Spoon potato mixture into a 9- x 13-inch pan that has been buttered or sprayed with nonstick cooking spray. Sprinkle with paprika and chives or parsley. Bake, uncovered, for 30 minutes.

Serves 8 to 10

Save Time: Potatoes are much easier to peel if you boil them with their skins on and remove the peels after cooking.

RANCH POTATOES

Kids love Ranch dressing. This recipe where it flavors potatoes is sure to be a favorite.

FOR POTATOES:

8 to 10	medium red potatoes, cooked and quartered (peeled, if desired)
½	cup sour cream
½	cup Ranch dressing
3 or 4	sliced cooked and crumbled bacon
2	tablespoons minced fresh parsley
1½	cups grated cheddar cheese, divided

FOR OPTIONAL TOPPING:

2	cups crushed corn flakes
¼	cup butter, melted

Heat oven to 350° F.

Arrange quartered potatoes in a 9- x 13-inch pan that has been greased or sprayed with nonstick cooking spray. In a small bowl, combine sour cream, Ranch dressing, bacon, parsley, and 1 cup cheese. Spread sour cream mixture over potatoes and gently toss. Top with ½ cup cheese.

If making optional topping, combine corn flakes and butter. Sprinkle over casserole. Bake, uncovered for 40 to 45 minutes.

Serves 8

CREAMY POTATOES

Put these potatoes in your slow cooker in the morning and enjoy them for dinner in the evening.

2 to 3 pounds small red potatoes, quartered, or russet potatoes, peeled and quartered
1 package (8 ounces) cream cheese, softened
1 envelope ranch salad dressing mix
1 can (10¾ ounces) cream of potato soup

Place potatoes in a slow cooker. In a small bowl, combine cream cheese, salad dressing mix, and soup. Pour over potatoes. Cover; cook on low heat for 7 to 8 hours or on high heat for 3½ to 4½ hours.

Serves 6 to 8

OVEN-ROASTED POTATOES

For a variation, replace the rosemary with any favorite herb or combination of herbs that you enjoy.

12 to 14	medium to large new potatoes, peeled, or 6 to 8 russet potatoes, peeled
½	cup butter
¼	cup olive oil
1 to 2	tablespoons dried rosemary
1	teaspoon salt
½	teaspoon pepper

Cook potatoes in a large saucepan in lightly salted water about 15 to 20 minutes. Potatoes should still be firm and not overcooked. Drain potatoes and cool. Cut into chunks.

Heat oven to 375° F.

Place butter in a 9- x 13-inch baking dish or shallow roasting pan. Place pan in oven and melt butter about 3 to 5 minutes. Watch so that it does not burn; remove from oven. Add olive oil, rosemary, salt, and pepper; stir to mix. Add potatoes and turn them so that all pieces are coated. Return pan to oven and bake for 45 minutes to 1 hour, turning again once or twice during cooking.

Serves 8 to 10

POTATO CAKES

Prepare extra mashed potatoes for one dinner, then you can make these wonderful potato cakes for another meal.

2	cups, or more, mashed potatoes, chilled
½	cup flour
1	teaspoon salt
½	teaspoon pepper
2	tablespoons olive oil
2	tablespoons butter

Form mashed potatoes into 8 patties, ½ inch thick. In a shallow bowl, mix flour, salt, and pepper. Heat oil and butter in a large skillet. Dip potato patties in flour mixture, coating both sides. Place in skillet and reduce heat to medium-low. Cook patties for 15 to 20 minutes, until a golden crust is formed. Turn over and cook on other side until golden, about 15 minutes more. Season with more salt and pepper to taste.

Serves 8

Variations: Add chopped onion, chives, parsley, cilantro, or grated cheese to chilled mashed potatoes.

ONION MASHED POTATOES

Potatoes are rich in complex carbohydrates, which provide vitamins, minerals, protein, and fiber.

6 to 8   potatoes, peeled and cut in quarters
1   envelope onion soup mix
½   cup milk
½   cup butter

In a large saucepan, cook potatoes in lightly salted water about 20 minutes. Drain. Add soup mix, milk, and butter. Mash potatoes with an electric mixer.

Serves 6 to 8

TWICE-BAKED POTATOES

Horseradish provides a little zip to these great old potatoes.

4 to 6	large baking potatoes
¼	cup butter
¼	cup milk
½ to 1	teaspoon salt
¼	teaspoon pepper
1 to 1½	teaspoons prepared horseradish (more, if desired)
2	tablespoons minced fresh parsley (optional)
¼	cup grated cheddar cheese

Heat oven to 350° F.

Wash potatoes and lightly pierce each with a fork. Bake for 60 to 75 minutes, until fork-tender. Cut each potato in half lengthwise. Carefully scoop out potato, leaving a thin shell.

In a large bowl, combine scooped out potato centers, butter, milk, salt, pepper, horseradish, and parsley, if desired. Beat with an electric mixer for 3 to 4 minutes until well blended and fluffy. Fill shells with potato mixture. Sprinkle with cheese and place on a baking sheet. Continue baking for 10 to 15 minutes, until cheese is melted and potatoes are heated through.

Serves 4 to 6

Save Time: Imitate time-consuming twice-baked potatoes by adding chopped green onions or white onion and grated cheddar cheese to mashed potatoes and then baking at 350° F for 15 to 20 minutes, or until heated through.

CHEESE POTATOES

These potatoes make a great side dish for a main-course meat, such as roast or chicken.

¼	cup flour
1	teaspoon salt
1½	cups milk
1	can (10¾ ounces) cream of celery soup
2	cups cheddar cheese, grated
5 to 6	large baking potatoes, peeled
1	cup chopped onion
	Paprika

Heat oven to 350° F.

In a medium saucepan, combine flour and salt. Gradually whisk in milk until mixture is smooth. Bring to a boil, cooking and stirring for 2 minutes. Remove from heat and whisk in soup and cheese until smooth.

Cut potatoes into 4 x ½ x ½ inch sticks. Place in a 9- x 13-inch baking pan that has been greased or sprayed with nonstick cooking spray. Sprinkle with onion. Top with cheese sauce. Bake for 55 to 60 minutes, or until potatoes are tender. Sprinkle with paprika.

Serves 8 to 10

SCALLOPED POTATOES

A sophisticated approach to old-fashioned scalloped potatoes.

5 or 6	large potatoes, peeled and thinly sliced
¾	cup light cream
1	cup milk
1	teaspoon salt
1	cup grated Gruyere, Swiss, or cheddar cheese
	Dash nutmeg

Heat oven to 350° F.

Place potatoes in a 9- x 13-inch baking dish or 3-quart casserole that has been buttered or sprayed with nonstick cooking spray. Pour cream and milk over the potatoes. Sprinkle with salt, cheese, and nutmeg. Bake, uncovered, for 50 to 60 minutes, until the potatoes are tender and most of the liquid is absorbed. Or, if preferred, bake potatoes before adding cheese and nutmeg. After 45 minutes, sprinkle cheese and nutmeg on potatoes and bake another 5 to 8 minutes, until cheese is melted.

Serves 6 to 8

Save Money: Use powdered milk to cook with; it is more economical and low-fat as well.

BAKED SWEET POTATOES

Often overlooked except on holidays, sweet potatoes provide variety and color on the dinner plate.

6 sweet potatoes
    Butter
    Cinnamon
    Brown sugar
    Maple Sour Cream

MAPLE SOUR CREAM

½ cup sour cream
1 tablespoon pure maple syrup
1 teaspoon minced jalapeño pepper or diced green chiles
1 teaspoon fresh lime juice
    Salt and pepper to taste

Heat oven to 400° F.

Wash skins of the sweet potatoes, then prick several places with a fork. Bake for about 40 to 50 minutes, until soft when tested. Cut in half lengthwise. Serve with butter, cinnamon, brown sugar or Maple Sour Cream as accompaniments.

To make Maple Sour Cream, mix sour cream, maple syrup, jalapeño pepper or green chiles, and lime juice in a small bowl. Season with salt and pepper.

Makes 6 servings

SPAGHETTI SQUASH

Spaghetti squash is simply a fun squash to cook!

1	spaghetti squash
1	clove garlic, minced
½	cup chopped onion
1	teaspoon basil
1	cup diced zucchini
2	tablespoons butter
1	cup chopped tomatoes
1	teaspoon salt
	Dash freshly ground pepper
1	cup grated mozzarella cheese

Heat oven to 400° F.

Pierce squash with a fork in several places and bake for 1 hour (like a baked potato). Cut open squash and remove seeds. Scrape baked squash into a 2½- or 3-quart casserole.

Sauté garlic, onion, basil, and zucchini in butter. Add to squash. Add tomatoes, salt, and pepper. Mix. Sprinkle with cheese. Microwave or bake in oven until cheese melts and mixture is warmed through.

Serves 6 to 8

Here's what to do with those plentiful zucchini growing in your or your neighbor's garden.

2	tablespoons butter or margarine
2	small zucchini, thinly sliced, or other summer squash, thinly sliced
1	medium onion, thinly sliced
2	medium tomatoes, sliced
½	teaspoon garlic salt
½	teaspoon basil
	Dash pepper
1	cup grated mozzarella cheese
1	cup seasoned croutons

Conventional Cooking Method: Melt butter in a large skillet. Add zucchini and onion. Cook over medium heat until crisp-tender. Gently stir in tomatoes, garlic salt, basil, and pepper. Cover; cook for 3 to 5 minutes until tomatoes are tender. Remove from heat; sprinkle with cheese and croutons. Cover; let stand for 2 to 3 minutes until cheese is melted.

Microwave Cooking Method: Place butter in a 2½ quart casserole dish or 9-inch square baking dish. Microwave on high for 30 seconds. Add zucchini and onion. Cook on high for 3 minutes. Gently stir in tomatoes, garlic salt, basil, and pepper. Cover and cook on high for 3 to 5 minutes. Sprinkle with cheese and croutons. Cover. Let stand 3 minutes, until cheese is melted.

Serves 4

*Try different assortments of vegetables with this superb
cheese sauce.*

1	large potato, peeled
1	zucchini, thickly sliced
⅓	cup diced green, red, or yellow pepper
1	cup broccoli florets
1	large carrot, sliced
¼	cup butter or margarine
¼	cup flour
1½	cups milk
½	teaspoon garlic salt
¼	teaspoon black pepper
½	cup grated cheddar or Swiss cheese
	Minced parsley (optional)

Cook potato in a small saucepan in boiling water until tender. Cut
into cubes.

Heat oven to 350° F.

In a large saucepan, cook zucchini; green, red, or yellow pepper; broccoli; and carrot in salted water until crisp-tender. Drain. Add potato.

In a medium saucepan, melt butter or margarine, and add flour, stirring
until smooth. Cook for 1 to 2 minutes. Gradually add milk, stirring until
mixture thickens. Add garlic salt, pepper, and cheese, stirring until
cheese melts.

Put vegetable mixture in a 2-quart baking dish or in individual baking
dishes. Pour sauce over vegetables. Sprinkle with parsley, if desired.
Bake for 15 to 20 minutes.

Serves 4 to 6

MARINATED VEGETABLES

Put together any group of vegetables you prefer for this excellent recipe.

½   cup lemon juice
½   cup olive oil
2   tablespoons sugar
2   teaspoons salt
½   teaspoon pepper
1½   teaspoons oregano
1   cup halved mushrooms
1   cup sliced carrots
½   red pepper, diced
½   yellow pepper, diced
1   cup diced tomatoes or cherry tomatoes, halved
1   cup broccoli, cut in florets and blanched
1   cup cauliflower, cut in florets and blanched
1   cup snow peas, trimmed and halved
1   small zucchini, sliced
½   cup sliced red onion

In a medium bowl or jar, whisk or shake lemon juice, olive oil, sugar, salt, pepper, and oregano. Put combination of mushrooms, carrots, red pepper, yellow pepper, tomatoes, broccoli, cauliflower, snow peas, zucchini, and red onion in a large resealable plastic bag. Pour dressing into bag and seal. Marinate in refrigerator for 6 hours or overnight, turning bag over several times. Drain marinade from vegetables and serve cold.

Serves 8 to 10

Family Tip: Have a fall harvest party. Make a dinner from your garden or from other locally grown produce. Invite extended family and/or friends.

231

ROASTED VEGETABLES

Time this recipe so that it can be served immediately. Goes well with grilled fish or chicken.

2	pounds small new potatoes, quartered
1	cup sliced carrots
1	red onion, cut in wedges
1½	tablespoons olive oil
2 to 3	cloves garlic, minced
3	tablespoons fresh lemon juice
1	teaspoon rosemary
1	teaspoon oregano
¾	teaspoon salt
½	teaspoon fresh ground black pepper
¾	teaspoon lemon pepper
1½ to 2	cups whole mushrooms
1	red pepper, cut in ½-inch strips
1	green pepper, cut in ½-inch strips
1	yellow pepper, cut in ½-inch strips

Heat oven to 450° F.

Spray a 9- x 13-inch baking pan with nonstick cooking spray. Place potatoes, carrots, and onion in pan. In a small bowl, stir together olive oil, garlic, lemon juice, rosemary, oregano, salt, pepper, and lemon pepper. Pour over potatoes, carrots, and onion, stirring to coat vegetables.

Bake for 30 minutes, stirring twice during cooking. Remove dish from oven and add mushrooms and peppers. Stir again to coat vegetables. Bake an additional 15 minutes.

Serves 8 to 10

Family Tip: For a change, spread the food out on the counter like a buffet and let each family member dish up his or her own dinner.

MUSTARD SAUCE FOR VEGETABLES

A creamy sauce for steamed carrots, cauliflower, asparagus, or broccoli.

2	tablespoons chopped onion
2	tablespoons butter
2	tablespoons flour
1	cup milk
1 to 1½	tablespoons Dijon mustard
1	tablespoon honey
½	teaspoon chicken bouillon granules

In a small saucepan, sauté onion in butter. Add flour and cook until light brown. Gradually add milk, stirring over medium heat until thick. Add mustard, honey, and bouillon and cook 1 more minute. Pour over steamed vegetables of choice.

Makes about 1 cup sauce

Save Money: Instead of buying baby carrots, buy whole carrots and wash and pare them yourself.

CHEESE SAUCE FOR VEGETABLES

This is the time for your favorite cheese to shine on just about any vegetable.

- ¼ cup butter
- ¼ cup flour
- ¼ teaspoon paprika
- ½ teaspoon dry mustard
- ¼ teaspoon black pepper
- ½ teaspoon salt
- 2 cups milk
- 1 cup grated cheese (such as cheddar, Swiss, Monterey Jack, or Mexican blend)

Melt butter in a medium saucepan. Stir in flour, paprika, mustard, pepper, and salt. Cook for 1 to 2 minutes. Gradually add milk, stirring constantly, until thickened. Add cheese, stirring until melted and thoroughly blended. Serve over your favorite steamed vegetables.

Makes 2 cups

Grilling

GRILLED KABOBS

If you use bamboo skewers, soak in water for 1 hour first to prevent burning on the grill.

FOR SAUCE:

1	bottle (9 ounces) oyster sauce
¼	cup soy sauce
¼	cup ketchup
2 to 3	cloves garlic, finely minced
¼	cup sugar
2	tablespoons olive oil

FOR KABOBS:

Boneless, skinless chicken breasts, cut into small pieces or shrimp, cleaned and deveined
Whole mushrooms
Green, red, yellow, or orange bell peppers, cut in medium pieces
Red or white onion, cut in wedges
Pineapple chunks or fresh pineapple, cut in chunks
Olives

In a small bowl, combine oyster sauce, soy sauce, ketchup, garlic, sugar, and oil; mix well.

Thread chicken, shrimp, mushrooms, peppers, onion, pineapple, or olives, as desired, on skewers. Brush sauce on kabobs and place on grill. Grill on medium heat, brushing several times with sauce, until shrimp or chicken is cooked through.

Variable servings

Save Time: Buy precut vegetables at the supermarket salad bar if you're short of time to chop vegetables for grilling or stir-frying.

BARBECUED RIBS

The mustard sauce in this recipe is a tasty alternative to the usual tomato-based sauces for ribs.

4	pounds pork spareribs or beef back ribs
2	cloves garlic, minced
1	teaspoon salt
½	teaspoon pepper
½	cup brown sugar
⅓	cup pure maple syrup or molasses
¼	cup spicy brown or Dijon mustard
¼	cup cider vinegar

Heat oven to 325° F.

Put ribs on a rack in a shallow roasting or baking pan. Rub garlic on ribs and sprinkle with salt and pepper. Bake, uncovered, for 1 hour for spareribs or 45 minutes for beef back ribs. Remove from oven.

Make Mustard Sauce by mixing maple syrup or molasses, mustard, and vinegar together in a small bowl. Brush sauce over spareribs and place on an oiled grill. Grill on medium heat about 10 minutes, turn, and baste with sauce again. Continue turning and basting until meat is cooked to desired doneness, about 15 to 20 minutes.

Serves 6 to 8

GRILLED PORK TENDERLOIN

Once you are introduced to pork tenderloin, you will want to cook it in numerous ways. This is a great grilled method.

1	cup Yoshida's Sauce
½	cup orange juice
¼	cup brown sugar
1	teaspoon dried basil
¼	teaspoon pepper
½	teaspoon ginger
1	teaspoon dry mustard
1 to 2	cloves garlic, minced
3 to 4	pounds pork tenderloins

Mix Yoshida's Sauce, orange juice, brown sugar, basil, pepper, ginger, mustard, and garlic in a glass baking dish or resealable plastic bag. Pierce tenderloins with a fork and place in marinade. Marinate for 1 to 3 hours in refrigerator.

Remove tenderloins from marinade; discard marinade. Place on oiled grill. Grill over medium-high heat for 20 minutes, or until inside is no longer pink. Slice thin.

Serves 8 to 10

HONEY-MUSTARD SALMON

This flavorful sauce keeps the salmon moist.

1	cup mayonnaise
¼ to ⅓	cup honey
2	teaspoons prepared mustard
1	tablespoon lemon juice
1	clove garlic, minced
4 to 6	salmon fillets
	Salt and pepper to taste
1 to 2	tomatoes, chopped
¼	cup chopped fresh basil (more, if desired)

In a small bowl, combine mayonnaise, honey, mustard, lemon juice, and garlic. Mix well.

Spray a large piece of heavy-duty aluminum foil or 2 stacked sheets of regular foil with cooking spray. Lay salmon on foil. Sprinkle with salt and pepper. Spread sauce over salmon. Distribute tomatoes and basil on top. Fold over foil and seal well. Grill on medium-high heat for 20 minutes.

Serves 4 to 6

Family Tip: Sing while you prepare dinner or do the dishes together.

HALIBUT WITH TOMATO SALSA

If you don't want to fire up the grill, bake or poach the halibut instead.

FOR HALIBUT:

- 2 tablespoons olive oil
- 1 tablespoon lime juice
- 1 tablespoon minced cilantro
- 4 halibut fillets or steaks
  Salt and pepper

FOR SALSA:

- 2 large tomatoes, diced
- 2 tablespoons chopped green onions
- 2 tablespoons minced cilantro
- 1 to 2 cloves garlic, minced
- 1 tablespoon olive oil
- 2 teaspoons lime juice
- 2 to 3 colored bell peppers (green, red, yellow), chopped
- 1 to 2 tablespoons diced green chiles or minced jalapeño pepper

Combine olive oil, lime juice, and cilantro in a glass baking dish or resealable plastic bag. Marinate halibut in mixture for 1 to 2 hours, but no longer as fish marinated too long falls apart.

To make salsa, combine tomatoes, green onions, cilantro, garlic, olive oil, lime juice, bell peppers, and jalapeño pepper or green chiles.

Remove halibut from marinade and sprinkle lightly with salt and pepper. Grill 6 to 8 minutes per side or until halibut is opaque and flakes easily. Serve with salsa.

Serves 4

GRILLED SWORDFISH WITH SALSA

Swordfish might sound exotic, but it is a mild, delicious fish. Serve with one of these salsas.

FOR SWORDFISH:

4 to 6   swordfish steaks, 1 inch thick
2 to 3   tablespoons olive oil
      Salt and pepper to taste

FOR PINEAPPLE-ORANGE SALSA:

1   cup diced fresh pineapple
1   orange, peeled, sectioned, and cut into chunks
1   mango, diced
¼   cup orange juice
1   tablespoon lemon juice
2   tablespoons minced jalapeño pepper or diced green chiles (or to taste)
1   tablespoon diced red pepper
2   green onions, chopped
2   tablespoons minced fresh cilantro

FOR MELON SALSA:

1   cup finely diced cantaloupe
1   cup finely diced honeydew melon
1   cup finely diced Crenshaw melon or watermelon
¼   cup lime juice
2   green onions, thinly sliced or 2 tablespoons diced red onion
2   tablespoons minced jalapeño pepper or diced green chiles (to taste)
2   tablespoons minced fresh cilantro

Brush swordfish with olive oil. Season with salt and pepper. Grill or broil about 12 minutes, turning fish once. Serve with Pineapple-Orange Salsa or Melon Salsa.

To make Pineapple-Orange Salsa, in a medium bowl, combine pineapple, orange, mango, orange juice, lemon juice, jalapeño pepper or green chiles, red pepper, green onions, and cilantro. Refrigerate before serving.

To make Melon Salsa, in a medium bowl, combine cantaloupe, honeydew melon, Crenshaw melon or watermelon, lime juice, onion, jalapeño pepper or green chiles, and cilantro. Refrigerate before serving.

Serves 4 to 6

ROSEMARY STEAK

Some people think of grilling outdoors in the summer only, but you can barbecue year-round—regardless of the weather.

¼	cup olive oil
⅓	cup lemon juice
1	teaspoon grated lemon peel
3	tablespoons Worcestershire sauce
1	clove garlic, minced
1	tablespoon fresh or 1 teaspoon dried rosemary
1	teaspoon salt
¼	teaspoon freshly ground pepper
4 to 6	steaks (sirloin, New York, rib-eye, T-bone, top round, or flank)

In a small bowl, combine olive oil, lemon juice, lemon peel, Worcestershire sauce, garlic, rosemary, salt, and pepper. Put steaks in a resealable plastic bag or glass baking dish. Add marinade. Marinate steak in refrigerator for 4 to 6 hours.

Grill steak over medium heat 12 to 15 minutes, to desired doneness.

Serves 4 to 6

LONDON BROIL

London Broil is actually a thick-cut top round steak and needs to be marinated for tenderness.

1	cup beef broth
½	cup soy sauce
¼	cup chopped onion or green onions
1	clove garlic, minced
2	tablespoons brown sugar
3	tablespoons lemon juice
2 to 2½	pounds London broil

In a small bowl, stir together beef broth, soy sauce, onion, garlic, brown sugar, and lemon juice. Place meat in a resealable plastic bag or a glass baking dish; add marinade. Cover and marinate in refrigerator 6 to 8 hours or overnight, turning several times.

Remove meat from marinade; discard marinade. Place on grill over medium heat. Grill about 10 minutes per side, until desired doneness. Slice diagonally in thin slices.

Serves 6 to 10

Save Time: To clean a barbecue grill rack, spray with oven cleaner (outdoors). Place rack in a clean plastic garbage bag and close the bag. Let stand overnight. The grime on the rack will come off easily.

HONEY LIME STEAK

A tantalizing marinade for a great backyard barbecue.

1	can (14½ ounces) beef broth
2	tablespoons brown sugar
1	tablespoon honey
¼	cup soy sauce
¼	cup lime juice
3 to 4	green onions, chopped
1	clove garlic, minced
1½ to 2	pounds steak (sirloin, New York, rib-eye, T-bone, top round, or flank), cut in serving size pieces

In a small bowl, mix together beef broth, brown sugar, honey, soy sauce, lime juice, green onions, and garlic. Put steak in a resealable plastic bag or glass baking dish. Add marinade. Marinate, covered, in refrigerator 4 to 6 hours.

Grill steak over medium heat 12 to 15 minutes, to desired doneness.

Serves 4 to 6

Family Tip: Have a "drive-in" movie night. Make your barbecue outdoors, then have everyone bring their plates into the family room and sit on the couch, chairs, or on the floor to watch a favorite video or DVD.

MARINATED STEAK

Grilling in the backyard and eating dinner with your family on the deck or patio are simple pleasures of summer.

½	cup olive oil
¼	cup Worcestershire sauce
¾	cup soy sauce
⅓	cup vinegar
1	cup lemon juice
2	tablespoons dried parsley flakes
¼	teaspoon garlic powder
1½ to 2	pounds steak (flank, top round, sirloin, T-bone, rib-eye, New York)

Mix oil, Worcestershire sauce, soy sauce, vinegar, lemon juice, parsley flakes, and garlic powder in a small bowl. Put marinade in a glass pan or resealable plastic bag. Place steak in marinade and cover. Marinate in refrigerator 6 to 8 hours or overnight. Remove steak from marinade and grill on barbecue, about 12 to 15 minutes, or until desired doneness.

Serves 4 to 6

Save Money: Compare price per unit (ounce or pound) of various brands as you grocery shop.

SESAME GINGER STEAK

Sesame seeds, sesame oil, and ginger give this steak its distinctive flavor.

¼	cup sesame seeds, toasted
2	teaspoons minced ginger
⅓	cup soy sauce
2	tablespoons sesame oil
¼	cup brown sugar
¼	cup chopped green onions
½	cup chopped onion
1	clove garlic, minced
¼	teaspoon pepper
2 to 3	pounds steak (sirloin, New York, rib-eye, T-bone, top round, or flank)

Place sesame seeds in a baking pan or pie plate and bake 5 to 6 minutes at 350° F, watching so they don't burn. (Or use purchased toasted sesame seeds.)

In a small bowl, combine sesame seeds, ginger, soy sauce, sesame oil, brown sugar, green onions, onion, garlic, and pepper. Pierce steak with a fork on both sides. Place steak in a glass baking dish or resealable plastic bag. Add marinade. Marinate in refrigerator for 4 hours or more.

Remove steak from marinade and grill over medium heat to desired doneness.

Serves 4 to 6

Cooking Tip: Marinades should be placed in a glass dish or heavy plastic bag rather than a metal dish or bowl to avoid a reaction between the acid in the marinade and the metal.

BEST BURGERS

The spice makes this burger.

1	pound ground beef
¼	cup quick-cooking or old-fashioned oats
1	egg
3½	teaspoons (or more) Montreal Steak Spice
	Hamburger buns or sandwich rolls

In a large bowl, mix together ground beef, oats, egg, and spice. Form into 4 patties. Grill patties over medium heat 10 to 15 minutes, turning once, until center of hamburger reaches desired doneness. Serve on hamburger buns or sandwich rolls with choice of condiments. (Hamburgers can also be broiled or fried.)

Serves 4

Family Tip: Create a family cookbook by inviting children, grandchildren, aunts, uncles, cousins, or other relatives to contribute recipes. Share your favorite recipes, writing about any traditions involved with the recipes. Cooking from the cookbook can bring your family closer together when distance separates you.

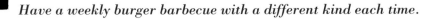

"HAVE IT YOUR WAY" BURGERS

Have a weekly burger barbecue with a different kind each time.

FOR MEXICAN BURGERS:

1½   pounds ground beef
1   package taco seasoning mix
     Grated Mexican blend cheese

FOR ITALIAN BURGERS:

1½   pounds ground beef
3   tablespoons Italian salad dressing
     Grated Parmesan cheese or sliced mozzarella cheese

FOR TEXAS BURGERS:

1½   pounds ground beef
3   tablespoons barbecue sauce
     Sliced cheddar cheese

FOR CALIFORNIA BURGERS:

1½   pounds ground beef
1   package Savory Herb with Garlic soup mix
     Sliced Monterey Jack cheese

Mix ground beef and desired seasonings in a large bowl. Shape into 6
patties. Grill patties over medium heat 10 to 15 minutes, turning once,
until center of hamburger reaches desired doneness. Add cheese during
last minute of grilling.

Serve on hamburger buns with desired condiments, including lettuce,
sliced tomatoes, and sliced onion.

Serves 6

CHILI LIME CHICKEN

For food safety, be sure to marinate chicken in the refrigerator and discard marinade after use.

½	cup lime juice
⅓	cup soy sauce
¼	cup olive oil
2	tablespoons sugar
1	tablespoon oregano
1	tablespoon fresh rosemary or 1 teaspoon dried rosemary
½	teaspoon chili powder
¼	teaspoon cayenne pepper (more, if desired)
1 to 2	cloves garlic, minced
8	boneless, skinless chicken breasts

In a medium bowl, combine lime juice, soy sauce, oil, sugar, oregano, rosemary, chili powder, cayenne pepper, and garlic. Put chicken breasts in a large resealable plastic bag or covered glass dish. Marinate 4 to 6 hours in the refrigerator.

Remove chicken from marinade and grill over medium heat 20 to 25 minutes, until center is cooked. Or bake in a large baking dish at 375° F for 30 minutes.

Serves 8

MAPLE CHICKEN

Pure maple syrup costs more than maple-flavored syrup, but the taste is worth it, and this recipe requires it.

- 1 cup pure maple syrup or honey
- 1 cup olive oil
- 2 tablespoons brown sugar
- 1 tablespoon red wine vinegar
- 1 tablespoon oregano
- 2 cloves garlic, minced
- 8 boneless, skinless chicken breasts or bone-in breasts

In a glass baking dish or resealable plastic bag, combine maple syrup or honey, oil, brown sugar, vinegar, oregano, and garlic. Add chicken. Cover and marinate in refrigerator for 3 to 4 hours. Remove chicken from marinade; discard marinade. Grill over medium heat for about 20 to 25 minutes, turning several times, until chicken is cooked in center.

Serves 8

Family Tip: Hold a fun dinner once a month during the year. Start off with something special on New Year's Day. Plan the dinner around holidays, birthdays, special occasions, or just a day that you designate.

CARIBBEAN CHICKEN

This recipe brings to mind those beautiful white sand beaches and intense turquoise waters.

1 to 2	cloves garlic, minced
1	teaspoon salt
½	teaspoon oregano
¼	teaspoon pepper
¼	cup olive oil
¼	cup red wine vinegar
1	teaspoon lemon juice
4	boneless, skinless chicken breasts

FOR PINEAPPLE SALSA:

1	can (20 ounces) pineapple chunks or 2 cups diced fresh pineapple
¼	cup olive oil
1	clove garlic, minced
2	tablespoons fresh lime juice
¼	teaspoon crushed red pepper flakes
1	teaspoon sugar
¼	cup diced red or green bell pepper
¼	cup diced red onion
1	jalapeño pepper, minced
2	tablespoons minced cilantro
	Salt and pepper to taste

In small bowl, combine garlic, salt, oregano, pepper, oil, vinegar, and lemon juice. Put marinade in a resealable plastic bag or glass dish, reserving 1 tablespoon. Add chicken. Marinate, covered, in refrigerator 1 hour.

Remove chicken from marinade. Cook chicken on grill on medium heat, turning once, for 20 to 25 minutes. Serve with salsa.

In a medium bowl, combine all ingredients for salsa and add reserved marinade.

Serves 4

POTATO PACKETS

*Let these potatoes cook on the grill while you're preparing the
rest of dinner.*

6   medium potatoes, peeled and thinly sliced
1   medium onion, sliced
6   tablespoons butter or margarine
½   cup grated cheddar cheese
2   tablespoons minced fresh parsley
1   tablespoon Worcestershire sauce
    Salt and pepper
1   cup chicken broth

Arrange potato and onion slices on a 20-inch square of heavy-duty
aluminum foil. Cut butter in small pieces and put on potatoes and
onions. Mix cheese, parsley, and Worcestershire sauce in a small bowl
then spread on potatoes. Sprinkle with salt and pepper to taste. Fold foil
up around potatoes. Sprinkle chicken broth over all. Tightly seal foil.

Grill, covered, over medium heat for 25 to 30 minutes, or until potatoes
are done.

Serves 4 to 6

*Family Tip: Hold a monthly birthday dinner to cele-
brate the birthdays of all family members (or
extended family members) who were born that
month. Rotate hosts or locations if desired and make
the dinner potluck for simplicity.*

GRILLED VEGGIES ON FOCCACIA BREAD

You'll relish this gourmet sandwich.

- ¼ cup mayonnaise
- 2 cloves garlic, minced
- 1 tablespoon fresh lemon juice
- 2 tablespoons olive oil
- 1 small red pepper, sliced
- 1 small zucchini, sliced
- 1 small red onion, sliced
- 4 ounces large mushrooms, sliced
- 1 small crookneck or summer squash, sliced

  Foccacia bread, sliced horizontally in 8 to 12 slices
- ½ cup bleu, feta, or gorgonzola cheese, crumbled

In a small bowl, mix mayonnaise, garlic, and lemon juice; set aside. Heat the grill to high.

Brush a small-screened grate or grill basket with olive oil. Brush red pepper, zucchini, red onion, mushrooms, and squash with olive oil. Grill vegetables about 3 to 4 minutes. Turn with tongs and grill another 3 to 4 minutes.

Brush foccacia bread slices with mayonnaise mixture. Arrange grilled vegetables on bread. Sprinkle with cheese. Put second slice of bread on top of vegetables.

Serves 4 to 6

Save Time: Buy packages of already cut and mixed coleslaw and salad greens.

GRILLED VEGETABLES

Grilling enhances the natural goodness of vegetables. Be sure to use a grill basket or rack.

Use an assortment of vegetables, such as:

2	zucchini, cut in chunks or thick slices
2	yellow squash, cut in chunks or thick slices
1	red, yellow, or green bell pepper, cut in chunks or thick slices
1	bunch asparagus (parboiled in water for 3 to 5 minutes)
1	cup mushrooms
1 to 2	onions, cut in wedges
10 to 12	red or new potatoes, halved or quartered (parboiled in water for 5 to 8 minutes)
1	cup cherry or plum tomatoes
	Olive oil (optional)
	Salt (optional)
	Herbs of Provence (optional)
	Thyme (optional)
	Basil (optional)
	Balsamic vinaigrette (optional)
2	eggs (optional)
1	cup bread crumbs (optional)
	Parmesan cheese (optional)

Prepare vegetables using one of the following methods.

METHOD 1

Put vegetables in a bowl and toss with a little olive oil. Sprinkle with a little salt. Then sprinkle with Herbs of Provence, thyme, basil, or any herb or spice desired. Put vegetables in an oiled grill basket or on an oiled grill rack. Grill over medium to high heat, about 10 minutes, until browned on the outside and tender when pierced with a fork. (Grilling time will vary depending on size, kind, and number of vegetables.)

METHOD 2

Brush or toss vegetables balsamic vinaigrette. Put vegetables in an oiled grill basket or on an oiled grill rack. Grill over medium to high heat, about 10 minutes, until browned on the outside and tender when pierced with a fork. (Grilling time will vary depending on size, kind, and number of vegetables.) Note: These vegetables can be added to cooked penne pasta, adding more balsamic vinaigrette, for a quick and delicious salad.

METHOD 3

Beat 2 eggs in a shallow bowl and add 1 tablespoon water. In another shallow bowl place 1 cup bread crumbs. Dip vegetables in egg mixture, then in bread crumbs. Place in an oiled grill basket or on an oiled grill rack. Sprinkle with grated Parmesan cheese. Grill over medium to high heat, about 10 minutes, until browned on the outside and tender when pierced with a fork. (Grilling time will vary depending on size, kind, and number of vegetables.)

Serves 6 to 8

GARLIC BREAD

Put the bread on the edge of the grill while your meat is cooking center stage.

½	cup butter, softened
1	clove garlic, minced (or more to taste)
¼	cup grated Parmesan cheese
1	loaf French or sourdough bread

In a small bowl, mix together butter, garlic, and Parmesan cheese.

Slice bread into 1-inch slices without cutting through the crust. Spread butter mixture on both sides of bread slices. Wrap loaf in foil. With grill at medium heat, place loaf on edge of grill. Toast for about 10 minutes, turning once or twice, until heated through.

Serves 8 to 12

Desserts

CHOCOLATE BREAD PUDDING

Serve with a scoop of vanilla ice cream, warmed white chocolate sauce, or whipped cream.

1	cup heavy cream
¾	cup sugar
¼	teaspoon salt
1	package (12 ounces) semisweet chocolate chips
2	eggs
2	egg yolks
2	cups milk
1	tablespoon vanilla
6 to 7	cups bread cubes made from heavy white bread (not sandwich bread), with crusts removed, cut into 1-inch cubes

Put cream, sugar, and salt in a heavy saucepan. Bring to a boil over medium heat, stirring constantly. Remove from heat and add chocolate chips. Let stand 2 minutes, then stir until smooth.

In a large bowl, whisk together eggs and egg yolks. Add milk and vanilla. Stir in the chocolate mixture; then stir in bread cubes. Refrigerate for 1 to 2 hours, gently stirring and pressing down bread cubes several times so that liquid is absorbed.

Heat oven to 325° F.

Butter a shallow 2-quart baking dish. Transfer pudding to dish and smooth top. Place dish in a water bath (a larger baking pan in which the pudding dish is set; add water to larger pan so that it comes partway up sides of pudding dish). Bake for 55 to 65 minutes, until center feels firms when pressed. Serve warm or cool.

Serves 9 to 12

Save Time: Chill cream before whipping. Try chilling the bowl and beaters, too. The colder they are, the quicker the cream whips.

RASPBERRY BREAD PUDDING WITH VANILLA SAUCE

A fabulous dessert for Sunday dinner or a special occasion.

FOR BREAD PUDDING:

4	cups heavy cream
2¾	cups sugar
1	egg
1	teaspoon vanilla
6 to 7	cups bread cubes made from heavy white bread (not sandwich bread), with crusts removed, cut into 1-inch cubes

FOR RASPBERRY FILLING:

4½ to 5	cups frozen or fresh raspberries
1	cup sugar
½	cup apple or orange juice

FOR VANILLA SAUCE:

1¼	cups butter
5	tablespoons flour
¼	teaspoon salt
3	cups heavy cream
⅓	cup sugar
2	teaspoons vanilla

Heat oven to 375° F.

In a very large bowl, mix cream, sugar, egg, and vanilla. Add bread cubes, stirring to mix. Let stand ½ hour, stirring 4 to 5 times, to allow bread to absorb cream.

In another large bowl, combine raspberries, sugar, and apple or orange juice.

Spray a 9- x 13-inch pan with nonstick cooking spray. Place three-fourths of bread mixture in pan. Spread raspberry filling over bread. Top with remaining bread mixture. Bake for 40 minutes. Serve warm with vanilla sauce.

260

To make Vanilla Sauce, in a heavy saucepan, melt butter over medium heat. Add flour and stir 5 to 8 minutes until mixture is golden in color, but not brown. Add salt, cream, and sugar, and cook until mixture is thickened. Remove from heat and add vanilla.

Serves 8 to 12

CHOCOLATE MOUSSE

Frozen whipped topping can be used in place of whipping cream.

1	large package instant chocolate pudding mix
3	cups milk
½	cup powdered sugar
1½	cups whipping cream, whipped

In a large bowl, mix pudding and milk, stirring until it begins to thicken. Refrigerate until thickened about 10 to 15 minutes. Stir powdered sugar and 2½ cups whipped cream into pudding. Spoon into individual dessert dishes. Serve with a dollop of remaining ½ cup whipped cream.

Serves 6

Family Tip: Make your Valentine's Day dinner a celebration of love. Ask everyone to wear red. Bake heart-shaped cookies with each person's name written in frosting and set the cookies on the tables as place cards. Put each family member's name on a slip of paper and put them in a jar on the table. During the dinner, have each family member draw a name and say something he or she loves about that person. (If you draw your own name, put it back and try again.) 261

LEMON PUDDING CAKE

For a variation, try lime juice and lime zest in place of lemon for a different flavor.

2	eggs, separated
1½	teaspoons grated lemon peel
¼	cup fresh lemon juice
⅔	cup milk
1	cup sugar
¼	cup flour
½	teaspoon salt

Heat oven to 350° F.

In a deep bowl, whip egg whites until stiff peaks form. Set aside. In a large bowl, beat egg yolks; then blend in lemon peel, lemon juice, and milk. Add sugar, flour, and salt. Mix until smooth. Fold egg whites into lemon mixture, blending with a spatula.

Spray an 8- x 8-inch pan with nonstick cooking spray.* Pour cake mixture into pan. Place this pan into a larger pan and set on oven rack. Pour enough hot water into large pan to measure approximately 1 inch. Bake for 45 to 50 minutes. Serve warm.

*Note: Recipe can be doubled and baked in a 9- x 13-inch pan.

Serves 6 to 9

Save Time: Quickly separate the egg yolk from the white with a funnel. Crack the egg into the funnel over a bowl. The white will drop into the bowl and the yolk will remain in the funnel.

CHOCOLATE PUDDING CAKE

You'll wonder how this combination results in a cake—but it does.

FOR CAKE:

1	cup flour
¾	cup sugar
2	teaspoons baking powder
½	teaspoon salt
3	tablespoons cocoa
½	cup milk
1	teaspoon vanilla
2	tablespoons butter, melted
½ to ¾	cup chopped walnuts or pecans
	Vanilla ice cream or whipped cream

FOR TOPPING:

½	cup sugar
½	cup brown sugar
2	tablespoons cocoa
1	cup boiling water

Heat oven to 350° F.

In a large bowl, stir together flour, sugar, baking powder, salt, and cocoa. Add milk, vanilla, and butter, and blend thoroughly. Stir in walnuts or pecans. Spoon mixture into an 8- x 8-inch pan that has been greased or sprayed with nonstick cooking spray.

To make Topping, combine sugar, brown sugar, cocoa, and water in a medium bowl and pour over unbaked batter.

Bake for 40 to 45 minutes. Cool slightly. Cut into squares and serve upside down with vanilla ice cream or whipped cream.

Serves 6 to 9

CARAMEL APPLE BARS

Caramel and apples—always a winning combination.

2	cups flour
1½	cups brown sugar
1	cup butter, softened
2	cups quick-cooking oats
1	teaspoon baking soda
1	jar (12½ ounces) caramel topping
½	cup flour
3	cups coarsely chopped, peeled apples
½	cup chopped walnuts or pecans

Heat oven to 350° F.

Grease a 10- x 15- x 1-inch baking pan or spray with nonstick cooking spray.

In a large bowl combine flour, brown sugar, butter, oats, and baking soda. Mix until crumbly. Press half of mixture (about 2½ cups) in pan. Bake for 8 minutes. Remove from oven.

While crust is baking, combine caramel topping and flour in a small saucepan. Bring to a boil over medium heat, stirring constantly. Reduce heat and cook until mixture slightly thickens.

Sprinkle apples and nuts on crust. Pour caramel over apples and nuts. Sprinkle reserved crumb mixture over top. Bake for 20 to 25 minutes, or until golden brown. Cool 30 minutes. Refrigerate another 30 minutes until set. Cut into bars.

Makes 2 dozen bars

PEANUT BUTTER BARS

An excellent treat for peanut butter lovers.

FOR BARS:

1	cup peanut butter (creamy or crunchy), divided
¾	cup butter, softened
¾	cup sugar
¾	cup brown sugar
2	eggs
1½	cups flour
1	teaspoon baking soda
1½	cups old-fashioned or quick-cooking oats
1	teaspoon vanilla
½	teaspoon salt

FOR CHOCOLATE FROSTING:

¼	cup butter, melted
⅓	cup cocoa
2 to 2½	tablespoons milk
½	teaspoon vanilla
2 to 3	cups powdered sugar

Heat oven to 350° F.

In a large bowl, cream ¾ cup peanut butter, butter, sugar, and brown sugar together until light and fluffy. Beat in eggs. Add flour, baking soda, oats, vanilla, and salt, mixing well.

Spread dough in a 9- x 13-inch pan. Bake for 15 to 17 minutes, or until edges start to brown. Remove from oven and spread with ¼ cup peanut butter, spreading over top as it melts. When cool, frost with chocolate frosting and cut into bars.

To make Chocolate Frosting, mix together butter, cocoa, milk, and vanilla. Beat in powdered sugar, about a cup at a time, until it reaches desired consistency.

Makes 2 dozen bars

CHOCOLATE CARAMEL BARS

For an even richer experience, serve these bars with a scoop of vanilla ice cream.

2	cups flour
2	cups quick-cooking oats
1½	cups brown sugar
1	teaspoon baking soda
½	teaspoon salt
1¼	cups unsalted butter, softened
1	jar (12½ ounces) caramel topping
3	tablespoons flour
1	cup semisweet chocolate chips
½	cup chopped pecans or walnuts

Heat oven to 350° F.

In a large bowl, combine flour, oats, brown sugar, baking soda, salt, and butter. Mix with an electric mixer on low speed until crumbly. Reserve 3 cups mixture.

Grease, spray with nonstick cooking spray, or line with parchment paper a 9- x 13-inch baking pan. Press remaining crumb mixture in pan. Bake for 10 minutes. Remove from oven.

While crust is baking, stir together caramel topping and flour in a small bowl.

Sprinkle chocolate chips and pecans over baked crust. Pour caramel on top. Sprinkle reserved 3 cups crumb mixture over caramel. Return pan to oven and bake for 22 to 25 minutes, until golden brown. Cool 1 to 3 hours before cutting.

Makes 2 dozen bars

BLACK-AND-WHITE BROWNIES

Brownies with style!

1¾	cups flour, divided
¼	cup brown sugar
½	cup butter, softened
1	cup mini or regular chocolate chips (coarsely chopped), divided
1⅓	cups sugar
½	cup cocoa
1½	teaspoons baking powder
½	teaspoon salt
3	eggs
1	cup butter, melted
1	tablespoon vanilla
½	cup chopped walnuts or pecans

Heat oven to 350° F.

In a medium bowl, mix together 1 cup flour and brown sugar. Using a fork or pastry blender, cut in softened butter until mixture is crumbly. Add ¼ cup chocolate chips. Press mixture into a 9-inch square or 7- x 11-inch baking pan that has been buttered, sprayed with nonstick cooking spray, or lined with parchment paper. Bake for 8 minutes.

In a large bowl, combine sugar, ¾ cup flour, cocoa, baking powder, and salt. Add eggs, melted butter, and vanilla. Mix until well blended. Add remaining ¾ cup chocolate chips and walnuts or pecans. Spread over crust in pan. Bake for 40 minutes. Cool. Cut into bars.

Makes 18 to 24 brownies

DOUBLE CHOCOLATE BROWNIES

Rich and chocolatey—who doesn't love a good brownie?

- ¾ cup flour
- ¼ teaspoon baking soda
- ¼ teaspoon salt
- 1 cup butter
- ¾ cup sugar
- 2 tablespoons water
- 1 package (12 ounces) semisweet chocolate chips, divided
- 1 teaspoon vanilla
- 2 eggs
- ½ cup chopped walnuts or pecans (optional)

Heat oven to 325° F.

In a small bowl, mix flour, baking soda, and salt; set aside. In a small saucepan or in a microwavable bowl, combine butter, sugar, and water. Bring just to a boil and remove from heat. Add 1 cup chocolate chips and vanilla; stir until chocolate is melted. Add eggs and flour mixture and blend. Stir in remaining 1 cup chocolate chips. Add nuts, if desired. Grease or spray a 9-inch square pan with nonstick cooking spray. Pour batter into pan and bake for 30 to 35 minutes. Cool completely before cutting.

Makes 1 dozen brownies

Family Tip: Discuss books during mealtime. Ask family members to share their current and longtime favorites.

FOUR-CHIP BROWNIES

Brownies and a tall glass of cold milk are sure to be a hit with your family.

¾	cup flour
¼	teaspoon baking soda
½	teaspoon salt
⅓	cup butter, softened
¾	cup sugar
2	tablespoons water
1	package (6 ounces) semisweet chocolate chips
2	eggs
½	cup vanilla milk chips
½	cup milk chocolate chips
⅓	cup butterscotch chips
½	cup chopped pecans or walnuts

Heat oven to 325° F.

In a small bowl, stir together flour, baking soda, and salt. In a medium saucepan, combine butter, sugar, and water. Heat just to a boil. Remove from heat and add semisweet chocolate chips. Stir until chocolate is melted and mixture is smooth. Add eggs, one at a time, beating after each addition. Blend in flour mixture.

Stir in vanilla milk chips, milk chocolate chips, butterscotch chips, and pecans or walnuts. Spread into an 8-inch square pan that has been greased or sprayed with nonstick cooking spray. Bake for 30 to 35 minutes. Cool. Cut into 2-inch squares.

Makes 16 brownies

ROCKY ROAD BROWNIES

If you like Rocky Road ice cream, you'll love these brownies.

FOR BROWNIES:

1	cup butter, melted
2	cups sugar
⅓	cup cocoa
4	eggs
1½	cups flour
	Dash salt
1	teaspoon vanilla
1½	cup nuts
2½	cups miniature marshmallows

FOR FROSTING:

½	cup butter, melted
½	cup cocoa
1	teaspoon vanilla
	Dash salt
2 to 2½	cups powdered sugar
¼	cup half-and-half or evaporated milk

In a large bowl, combine butter, sugar, and cocoa. Mix well. Add eggs, one at a time, beating well after each addition. Blend in flour, salt, and vanilla. Stir in nuts.

Pour batter into a greased 9- x 13-inch pan or spray with nonstick cooking spray. Bake for 25 minutes. Remove from oven. Cover with miniature marshmallows. Return to oven for 5 minutes longer. Cool, then frost.

In a medium bowl, combine melted butter and cocoa. Add vanilla and salt. Gradually add small amounts of powdered sugar and half-and-half or milk until of spreading consistency.

Makes 2 dozen brownies

WAFFLE BROWNIES

Great to throw together for the teenagers hanging around the kitchen on a Friday night. These brownies are best when eaten warm.

½   cup butter or margarine, melted
7   tablespoons cocoa
4   eggs, beaten
1½ cups sugar
2   cups flour
½   teaspoon salt
1   tablespoon vanilla
    Chocolate frosting (homemade or purchased)
    Chopped walnuts for topping (optional)
    Chocolate sprinkles for topping (optional)

In a large bowl, mix butter and cocoa. Add eggs and mix well. Add sugar, flour, salt, and vanilla; mix. Heat waffle iron to medium or high heat. Drop dough by tablespoonfuls on waffle iron (in each section) Cook for about 1 to 2 minutes.

Frost with chocolate frosting while warm. Top with nuts or sprinkles, if desired.

Makes 2 to 2½ dozen brownies

Family Tip: Make sure dinnertime belongs only to you. Let the home answering machine respond to phone calls, have family members turn off cell phones, and turn off the television.

BERRY BROWNIE TORTE

A rich and elegant dessert.

        1   package (about 20 ounces) fudge brownie mix
        1   can (14 ounces) sweetened condensed milk
        ½   cup water
        1   small package instant vanilla pudding mix
        1   cup whipping cream, whipped
    2 to 3   cups fresh or frozen raspberries or sliced strawberries
             (without syrup)

Heat oven to 350° F.

Spray 2 (9-inch) cake pans with cooking spray. Line with parchment
paper or foil, extending sides up. Spray paper or foil with cooking spray.
Prepare brownies according to package directions for cake-like brownies.
Divide batter into pans. Bake for 20 minutes; cool. Remove from pans.

In a large bowl, mix sweetened condensed milk with water. Beat in pudding mix; chill for 5 minutes. Fold in whipped cream. Place 1 brownie
layer on a serving plate. Top with half of pudding mixture. Arrange raspberries or strawberries on pudding mixture. Repeat layers. Cut in
wedges to serve.

Serves 8 to 10

ICE CREAM AND CAKE DESSERT

This dessert will be at the top of your "easy to make, but feels gourmet" list. For a variation, use a devil's food or chocolate cake mix, chopped pecans or walnuts, and strawberry, peppermint, or chocolate mint ice cream.

1 package (18¼ ounces) German chocolate cake mix
¾ cup butter, softened
½ cup brown sugar
1 cup chopped almonds
½ gallon burnt almond fudge ice cream, softened

Heat oven to 350° F.

In a large bowl, combine cake mix, butter, brown sugar, and almonds until well blended. Spread mixture on a 12- x 17-inch jelly-roll pan, pressing down until thin and even. Bake for 12 minutes. Remove from oven and let cool, then break into bite-size pieces.

In a 9- x 13-inch baking dish, place a layer of cake pieces. Spread half of the ice cream over cake. Add a second layer of cake pieces and then remainder of ice cream. Top with remaining cake pieces. Put covered pan in freezer and freeze about 4 hours, until hardened. Soften dessert 10 minutes before serving.

Serves 9 to 12

PIÑA COLADA CAKE

This cake is best when made the night before and refrigerated.

- 1   package (18¼ ounces) white or yellow cake mix
- 1   can (8 ounces) cream of coconut (not coconut milk)
- 1   can (20 ounces) crushed pineapple, drained
- 1   carton (8 ounces) Cool Whip or 1 pint whipping cream, whipped and sweetened

Bake cake in a 9- x 13-inch pan according to package directions. Remove cake from oven and immediately punch holes in it with the handle of a wooden spoon. While cake is hot, pour cream of coconut over the entire surface. Spoon a layer of crushed pineapple over cake. Refrigerate. When ready to serve cake, spread with Cool Whip or whipped cream.

Serves 9 to 12

Family Tip: Playing verbal games at the dinner table will help young children think creatively. It's also a lot of fun! Ask kids to name all the vegetables that begin with the letter B or to think of all the foods they like that are red. You could also tell the beginning of a story and then go around the table, letting each family member add to the story.

GINGER CAKE

Serve plain, with ice cream or whipped cream, sliced bananas, or a lemon sauce.

1	cup butter, softened
1½	cups sugar
3	eggs
¾	cup molasses
3¾	cups flour
1	teaspoon baking soda
1	teaspoon salt
2	teaspoons cinnamon
1	teaspoon cloves
1	teaspoon ginger
¾	cup milk

Heat oven to 350° F.

In a large bowl, cream butter and sugar. Add eggs, one at a time, beating until fluffy. Add molasses and mix well. Stir together or sift flour, baking soda, salt, cinnamon, cloves, and ginger. Add flour mixture to egg mixture alternately with milk, blending well.

Put batter in a 9- x 13-inch pan that has been greased or sprayed with nonstick cooking spray. Bake for 35 minutes, or until a toothpick inserted in the center comes out clean.

Serves 9 to 12

Family Tip: Don't make dinner a time to solve family problems or differences. Strive to make meals enjoyable experiences.

SIMPLE CHOCOLATE CAKE

Moist and delicious and almost as easy as a mix.

½	cup butter, softened
2	cups sugar
2	eggs
½	cup cocoa
2	teaspoons baking soda
2	teaspoons baking powder
2½	cups flour
½	teaspoon salt
2	cups boiling water
2	teaspoons vanilla
	Chocolate frosting (homemade or purchased)

Heat oven to 350° F.

In a large bowl, cream butter and sugar until light and fluffy. Beat in eggs.

In a medium bowl, stir together cocoa, baking soda, baking powder, flour, and salt. Add dry ingredients to butter mixture alternately with boiling water, beating after each addition. Add vanilla.

Pour batter into 2 (8- or 9-inch) cake pans that have been sprayed with nonstick cooking spray or lined with parchment paper and sprayed. Bake for 30 minutes. Remove from pans and cool. Place one layer on a serving plate. Spread chocolate frosting on top. Gently add second layer, pressing down slightly to set layers. Frost top and sides.

Serves 8 to 10

CREAMY CHOCOLATE FROSTING

A rich, creamy chocolate frosting.

   ¾   cup whipping cream
   1½   cups semisweet chocolate chips
   1   teaspoon vanilla
1 to 2   cups powdered sugar

In a medium saucepan, bring cream to a boil. Remove immediately and add chocolate chips, stirring until chips melt. Add vanilla. Mix in powdered sugar to make frosting of desired consistency.

Makes frosting for a 9-inch layer cake

Family Tip: Shake things up a bit at dinnertime. Instead of having family members sit in their traditional place, play musical chairs and sit somewhere new during dinner.

PINEAPPLE-ORANGE CAKE

A new kind of "fruit cake."

1 package (18¼ ounces) yellow or orange cake mix
4 eggs
¾ cup vegetable oil
1 can (11 ounces) mandarin oranges, undrained
1 can (20 ounces) crushed pineapple, drained and
   juice reserved
1 small package instant vanilla pudding mix
1 carton (8 ounces) Cool Whip, thawed

Heat oven to 350° F.

In a large bowl, combine cake mix, eggs, oil, and mandarin oranges with juice. Pour into a greased and floured 9- x 13-inch cake pan. Bake for 30 to 35 minutes. While cake is still warm, pour ¾ cup juice from pineapple over cake. Cool.

In a medium bowl, mix pineapple, pudding mix, and Cool Whip. Spread over cake. Keep refrigerated.

Serves 12

Family Tip: Take an annual family photo of a food tradition in your family, such as preparing Thanksgiving dinner, eating out on the patio during the summer, or warming up with chili after a day of skiing. Keep the photos together in a small album so that you can enjoy seeing the changes in your family over the years.

CHEESECAKE

A hard-to-resist but not-too-rich cheesecake. For a variation, substitute another pie filling or fresh fruit for the cherry pie filling.

- 1 package (18¼ ounces) yellow or white cake mix (reserve 1 cup)
- 2 tablespoons vegetable oil
- 4 eggs
- 2 packages (8 ounces each) cream cheese, softened
- ½ cup sugar
- 1½ cups milk
- 3 tablespoons lemon juice
- 1 teaspoon vanilla
- 1 can (30 ounces) cherry pie filling

Heat oven to 300° F.

Put cake mix (minus 1 cup), oil, and 1 egg in a large bowl. Mix until crumbly. Press mixture into a 9- x 13-inch pan that has been greased or sprayed with nonstick cooking spray.

In another large bowl, with an electric mixer blend cream cheese and sugar until well mixed. Add 3 eggs and reserved cake mix. Beat 1 minute at low speed, gradually adding milk, lemon juice, and vanilla. Blend until smooth. Pour mixture onto prepared crust.

Bake for 45 to 55 minutes, until center is firm. Cool to room temperature. Spread pie filling on cheesecake. Cover and chill 1 hour.

Serves 12

Save Time: Soften cream cheese quickly in the microwave. Unwrap cheese and discard foil, put on a microwave-safe plate, and heat for 1 minute at 50 percent power.

TOFFEE CAKE WITH CARAMEL SAUCE

Because this cake is so rich, it goes a long way.

FOR CAKE:

1½	cups water
1	cup chopped, pitted dates
2	teaspoons baking soda
2½	cups flour
2	teaspoons baking powder
1	cup butter
⅔	cup sugar
4	eggs
2	teaspoons vanilla
½	cup chopped pecans or walnuts (optional)

FOR CARAMEL SAUCE:

4	cups heavy cream
2	cups brown sugar
½	cup butter

In a small saucepan, combine water, dates, and baking soda. Bring to a boil, remove from heat, and cool.

In a small bowl, combine flour and baking powder. In a large bowl, cream butter and sugar until light and fluffy. Beat in eggs, one at a time. Mix in vanilla and half of flour mixture. Add date mixture, then remaining flour; mix well. Add pecans or walnuts, if desired. Pour into a buttered Bundt pan. (A silicone pan works best.)

Heat oven to 350° F. Bake for 45 minutes. While cake is baking, make Caramel Sauce by combining cream, brown sugar, and butter in a heavy saucepan. Bring to a boil and reduce heat. Cook about 6 minutes, stirring several times. After cake has baked 45 minutes, pour ¾ cup sauce over cake and bake 15 more minutes. Cool slightly and invert onto a platter. Slice and drizzle with remaining Caramel Sauce.

Serves 15 to 20

LEMON POUND CAKE

Serve solo or with fresh fruit and whipped cream.

1	package (8 ounces) cream cheese, softened
4	eggs
1	package (18¼ ounces) yellow cake mix
½	cup milk
1 to 1½	tablespoons grated lemon peel

Heat oven to 350° F.

In a large bowl, beat cream cheese until light and fluffy. Add eggs, one at a time, mixing well after each addition. Add cake mix alternately with milk, beating until smooth. Stir in lemon peel.

Pour batter into a 10-inch tube pan or Bundt pan that has been greased or sprayed with nonstick cooking spray. Bake for 55 minutes, or until a toothpick inserted in the center comes out clean.

Serves 12 to 15

Cooking Tip: If a piece of egg shell falls into your mixture, dip a larger piece of shell into the bowl. It adheres instantly.

SHORTCAKE

Fresh strawberries, raspberries, or sliced peaches make this shortcake a singular summer treat.

FOR SHORTCAKE:

1¼	cups flour
¾	cup sugar
⅓	cup butter
⅔	cup milk
2	eggs
2½	teaspoons baking powder
½	teaspoon salt
1	teaspoon vanilla
3 to 4	cups fresh fruit (or to taste)
	Whipped cream, Cool Whip, or other topping

FOR CHOCOLATE CREAM TOPPING:

1	cup whipping cream
½	cup powdered sugar
1	tablespoon cocoa
½	teaspoon vanilla

FOR SOUR CREAM TOPPING:

1	cup whipping cream
½	cup sour cream
1	cup powdered sugar
½	teaspoon vanilla

Heat oven to 400° F.

Combine flour, sugar, butter, milk, eggs, baking powder, salt, and vanilla in a large bowl. Beat at medium speed of electric mixer for 1 to 2 minutes. Pour batter into a greased and floured 5- x 9-inch loaf pan.

Bake for 20 to 25 minutes. Remove from pan and cool. Slice. Top with fresh fruit and whipped cream, Cool Whip, Chocolate Cream Topping, or Sour Cream Topping.

To make Chocolate Cream Topping, put whipping cream, powdered sugar, cocoa, and vanilla into a medium bowl. With an electric mixer, beat on high speed until cream is fluffy and forms soft peaks.

To make Sour Cream Topping, put whipping cream, sour cream, powdered sugar, and vanilla into a medium bowl. With an electric mixer, beat on high speed until cream is fluffy and forms soft peaks.

Serves 8 to 10

FROSTED ANGEL FOOD DESSERT

A delicious combination of light cake, creamy frosting, and fresh fruit.

1	carton (16 ounces) Cool Whip, thawed, or 1 cup (or more) whipping cream, whipped
1	package (8 ounces) cream cheese, softened
1 to 1½	cups powdered sugar
1	angel food cake (about 15 ounces)
	Sliced strawberries, raspberries, or sliced peaches

Mix Cool Whip, cream cheese, and powdered sugar together. Frost angel food cake. Chill. Slice and garnish with berries or peaches.

Serves 8 to 10

Save Time: To quickly peel fresh peaches or tomatoes, dip them in boiling water; peeling is only a matter of pulling the skins off.

CRANBERRY APPLE CRISP

Buy several extra bags of fresh cranberries at Thanksgiving and freeze for later uses, since cranberries are seasonal.

2	packages (12 ounces each) fresh or frozen cranberries
2½	cups chopped apples
2	tablespoons butter, cut in pieces
1¼	cups sugar
1	cup chopped pecans or walnuts
2	eggs, slightly beaten
½	cup butter, melted
1	cup sugar
¾	cup flour
	Vanilla ice cream or whipped cream

Heat oven to 325° F.

Spray a 9- x 13-inch baking pan with nonstick cooking spray. In a large bowl, toss together cranberries and apples. Spread in baking pan. Dot with butter. Sprinkle 1¼ cups sugar and pecans or walnuts over fruit.

In the bowl used to mix the fruit, mix together eggs, melted butter, sugar, and flour. Pour over cranberry mixture.

Bake for 1 hour, or until top is golden brown. Serve warm or at room temperature with vanilla ice cream or whipped cream.

Serves 12 to 15

CARAMEL APPLE CRISP

Does your family like caramel apples? Then they'll think this dessert is fabulous.

FOR APPLES:

8	cups peeled and sliced apples
1	cup brown sugar
2	tablespoons flour
½	cup milk
1	cup water

FOR TOPPING:

1⅓	cups flour
1	cup old-fashioned or quick-cooking oats
½	cup sugar
½	cup butter, softened
1	teaspoon salt
2	teaspoons cinnamon
2	small packages butterscotch pudding mix (either instant or cooked)
	Vanilla ice cream or whipped cream

Place sliced apples in a large bowl. Add brown sugar, flour, milk, and water; stir together. Spread in an ungreased 9- x 13-inch baking pan.

Heat oven to 350° F.

In a medium bowl, mix flour, oats, sugar, butter, salt, cinnamon, and pudding mix, until crumbly. Sprinkle over apples. Bake for 45 to 50 minutes, until golden brown. Serve with vanilla ice cream or whipped cream.

Serves 9 to 12

FRUIT COBBLER

This is probably the best fruit cobbler you've ever tasted!

FOR FRUIT:

4 to 5   cups fresh or frozen fruit (frozen mixed berries work well)
3 to 4   tablespoons butter
1   cup sugar
1   tablespoon cinnamon

FOR BATTER:

1½   cups sugar
½   cup butter, melted
1   teaspoon salt
2   teaspoons baking powder
2   cups flour
1   cup milk

FOR TOPPING:

½   cup sugar
1   tablespoon cornstarch
⅛   teaspoon salt
½   cup water

Heat oven to 325° F.

Spray a 9- x 13-inch pan with nonstick cooking spray. Spread fruit in pan; dot with butter. Sprinkle with sugar and cinnamon.

In a large bowl, combine 1½ cups sugar, melted butter, salt, baking powder, flour, and milk. Mix until smooth. Spread over fruit.

In a small bowl, mix ½ cup sugar, cornstarch, and salt. Sprinkle over batter. Pour water on top of batter. Bake for 1 hour.

Serves 12

PINEAPPLE CREAM DESSERT

An elegant dessert worthy of a special occasion.

FOR CRUST:

1½ cups flour
½ cup macadamia nuts or walnuts, finely chopped
¾ cup butter, softened

FOR PINEAPPLE CREAM FILLING:

1 can (20 ounces) crushed pineapple
¼ cup cornstarch
4 egg yolks
1 tablespoon water
1 cup sugar
¼ teaspoon salt
2 cups milk
2 tablespoons butter
1 teaspoon vanilla

FOR CREAM CHEESE FILLING:

1 package (8 ounces) cream cheese, softened
½ cup powdered sugar
½ teaspoon vanilla

FOR TOPPING:

1 cup whipping cream, whipped
¼ cup powdered sugar
2 tablespoons finely chopped macadamia nuts or walnuts
⅓ cup finely chopped macadamia nuts or walnuts
⅓ cup pineapple (reserved), drained

Heat oven to 375° F.

Mix flour, macadamia nuts or walnuts, and butter thoroughly. Press evenly into a 9- x 13-inch pan. Bake for 15 minutes until golden brown. Cool completely.

Measure 1 cup pineapple and juice. Combine cornstarch, egg yolks, and water in a small bowl. Combine sugar, salt, milk, and 1 cup pineapple and juice in a saucepan. Cook and stir on medium heat until mixture almost comes to a boil. Reduce heat to low. Add egg yolk mixture slowly, stirring constantly, and stir until thickened. Add butter and vanilla. Remove from heat; cover with waxed paper. Refrigerate for 30 minutes, stirring once or twice.

Drain juice from remaining pineapple. Combine cream cheese and powdered sugar; beat until blended and smooth. Add vanilla, macadamia nuts, and juice. Mix well. (If not of spreading consistency, add a tablespoon of milk.) Spread cream cheese filling over bottom of cooled baked crust. Cover with pineapple cream filling. Refrigerate until serving time.

Just prior to serving, spread with whipped cream mixed with powdered sugar. Garnish with remaining drained pineapple and macadamia nuts or walnuts.

Serves 12 to 15

Family Tip: Put on a theme dinner. Pretend that dinner is really a trip to the ski slopes, a fishing excursion, a night at a local team's basketball game, or an evening in a foreign city. Plan food, table setting, and decorations around the theme.

APPLESAUCE OATMEAL COOKIES

A classic favorite—coconut, chocolate chips, and toffee bits can also be added. Dates or dried cranberries may be substituted for the raisins.

2	cups sugar
1	cup butter
2	eggs, beaten
2	teaspoons soda
2	cups applesauce
2	teaspoons vanilla
3½	cups flour
2	teaspoons nutmeg
2	teaspoons cinnamon
1	teaspoon salt
2	cups quick-cooking or old-fashioned oats
2	cups raisins
2	cups walnuts or pecans
2	cups semisweet or milk chocolate chips (optional)
1	cup flaked coconut (optional)
1	cup toffee bits (optional)

Heat oven to 425° F.

Cream sugar and butter together in a large bowl. Add beaten eggs; mix until smooth. Add soda to applesauce and mix well. Add applesauce to sugar mixture, and then add vanilla.

Stir together flour, nutmeg, cinnamon, and salt. Add to applesauce mixture, mixing well. Add oats, raisins, and walnuts or pecans. Stir until batter is moist. Add optional ingredients, if desired. Drop by spoonfuls on a greased cookie sheet. Bake for 10 minutes, or until brown.

Makes 4 to 5 dozen cookies

GINGER SUGAR COOKIES

Soft and chewy—unlike ginger cookies from a box or package.

2	cups flour
2	teaspoons baking soda
1	teaspoon cinnamon
1	teaspoon ginger
1	teaspoon cloves
¼	teaspoon salt
1⅓	cups sugar, divided
¾	cup shortening
1	egg
¼	cup molasses (light or dark)
¾	cup sugar for rolling dough in

Heat oven to 375° F.

In a medium bowl, stir together flour, baking soda, cinnamon, ginger, cloves, salt, and ⅓ cup sugar.

In a large bowl, cream 1 cup sugar and shortening. Blend in egg and molasses. Add dry ingredients and mix until well blended. Shape dough into 1-inch balls. Roll in sugar, place on greased or sprayed cookie sheets, and press lightly. Bake for 8 to 10 minutes.

Makes 2½ dozen cookies

Save Time: When making Snickerdoodles or other cookies that are rolled in sugar, put sugar mixture in a small covered container or plastic resealable bag. Add, a few balls at a time, and shake.

HONEY COOKIES

You'll probably want to double this recipe as these cutout cookies disappear in a hurry.

⅓ cup shortening
1 cup sugar
1 egg
⅔ cup honey
2¾ cups flour
1 teaspoon baking soda
½ teaspoon salt
1 teaspoon vanilla

In a large bowl, cream shortening, sugar, egg, and honey. Add flour, baking soda, salt, and vanilla. Mix thoroughly.

Heat oven to 375° F.

Roll out dough on a floured surface, no thinner than ¼ inch thick. Cut in desired shapes with cookie cutters. Place cookies on a cookie sheet that has been greased or sprayed with nonstick cooking spray. Bake for 8 to 10 minutes, until lightly browned. Frost when cool.

Makes about 1½ to 2 dozen cookies

FOR FROSTING:

⅓ cup butter, melted
3 cups powdered sugar, divided
¼ cup milk, half-and-half, or evaporated milk
1 teaspoon vanilla, almond, or mint extract
2 to 3 drops food coloring (optional)

In a large bowl, combine butter and 1 cup powdered sugar with an electric mixer. Gradually add milk, half-and-half, or evaporated milk and remaining powdered sugar until frosting reaches spreading consistency. Add vanilla or other flavoring and food coloring, if desired.

PUMPKIN DROPS

Fall is in the air anytime of year with these soft and delicious pumpkin cookies.

½	cup butter, softened
1½	cups sugar
1	egg
1	cup canned pumpkin
1	teaspoon vanilla
2½	cups flour
1	teaspoon baking powder
1	teaspoon baking soda
1	teaspoon salt
1	teaspoon cinnamon
1	cup semisweet chocolate chips or raisins
½	cup chopped pecans or walnuts (optional)

Heat oven to 350° F.

In a large bowl, cream together butter and sugar until light and fluffy. Add egg, pumpkin, and vanilla. Mix or sift together flour, baking powder, baking soda, salt, and cinnamon. Add to pumpkin mixture, blending well. Stir in chocolate chips or raisins and pecans or walnuts, if desired.

Drop by spoonfuls on a cookie sheet that has been greased or sprayed with nonstick cooking spray. Bake for 15 minutes, or until golden brown.

Makes about 3 dozen cookies

HOMEMADE OREOS

Far better than the packaged kind.

1   package (18¼ ounces) devil's food cake mix
½   cup shortening
2   eggs

FOR VANILLA FROSTING:

¼   cup butter, softened
3   cups powdered sugar
3   tablespoons milk
1   teaspoon vanilla

FOR CREAM CHEESE FROSTING:

¼   cup butter, softened
2   packages (3 ounces each) cream cheese
3   cups powdered sugar
1½   teaspoons vanilla

Heat oven to 350° F.

In a large bowl, mix cake mix, shortening, and eggs with an electric hand mixer. Roll into walnut-sized balls. Place on a cookie sheet that has been greased or sprayed with nonstick cooking spray. Flatten slightly. Bake for 9 to 11 minutes. Cool. Frost half of the cookies with Vanilla Frosting or Cream Cheese Frosting. Place an unfrosted cookie on top of each frosted cookie.

To make Vanilla Frosting, in a large bowl, beat butter until fluffy. Beat in part of powdered sugar. Add milk and more powdered sugar until frosting reaches desired consistency. Add vanilla and mix well.

To make Cream Cheese Frosting, in a large bowl, beat butter and cream cheese together until well blended. Add powdered sugar until frosting reaches desired consistency. Add vanilla and mix well.

Makes about 20 to 22 cookies

CHOCOLATE TREASURES

Melt-in-your-mouth delights.

- 1   package (18¼ ounces) chocolate cake mix, any kind
- ½   cup butter or margarine, softened
- 1   egg
- 1   bag (12 ounces) Nestle Signature Treasure candies, unwrapped

Heat oven to 375° F.

In a large bowl, with an electric hand mixer mix together cake mix, butter, and egg. It will seem dry but keep mixing. Form dough around a Treasure candy and make into a ball that just covers it. Place on a cookie sheet that has been greased or sprayed with nonstick cooking spray and bake 9 to 10 minutes. Do not overbake!

Makes 2½ dozen cookies

Save Money: Collect manufacturers' coupons and use if final price is better than other brands.

Chocolate lovers will adore these cookies.

1	package (18¼ ounces) chocolate cake mix (any kind)
1	cup sour cream
1	small package instant chocolate pudding mix
2	eggs
1½	cups semisweet chocolate chips
¾	cup chopped walnuts (optional)

Heat oven to 350° F.

In a large bowl, blend cake mix, sour cream, pudding mix, and eggs. Beat until well combined and smooth. Add chocolate chips and walnuts, if desired. Drop by spoonfuls on a cookie sheet that has been greased or sprayed with nonstick cooking spray, placing at least 2 inches apart. Bake for 16 to 18 minutes, until centers are set but still soft. Cool cookies on cookie sheet 2 to 3 minutes before transferring to wire rack.

Makes 3 dozen cookies

Family Tip: Mix a large batch of cookies or several kinds at the same time. Put balls of cookie dough on a baking sheet and place them in the freezer. When dough is frozen, transfer balls to a freezer container and keep in freezer. Unthaw and bake as needed for fresh, homemade cookies.

COCONUT CHOCOLATE CHIP COOKIES

Destined to become one of your five-star cookie recipes.

1½ cups graham cracker crumbs
1   cup flour
2   teaspoons baking powder
1   can (14 ounces) sweetened condensed milk
½   cup butter, softened
1   cup flaked coconut
1   package (12 ounces) semisweet chocolate chips
½   package (6 ounces) milk chocolate chunks
1   cup chopped walnuts or pecans

Heat oven to 375° F.

In a small bowl, mix graham cracker crumbs, flour, and baking powder.

In a large bowl, beat condensed milk and butter until smooth. Add graham cracker mixture and beat well. Stir in coconut, chocolate chips, chocolate chunks, and walnuts or pecans.

Drop by spoonfuls on an ungreased cookie sheet. Bake for 9 to 10 minutes, until edges are lightly browned. Do not overbake.

Makes 2½ dozen cookies

OATMEAL CHOCOLATE CHIP COOKIES

Sure to be devoured by hungry children and their friends.
Parents love them too!

2	cups brown sugar
2	cups sugar
2	cups butter
4	eggs
2	teaspoons vanilla
2	teaspoons baking powder
2	teaspoons baking soda
1	teaspoon salt
4	cups flour
5	cups quick-cooking or old-fashioned oats
1	package (12 ounces) semisweet chocolate chips
1	package (10 ounces) toffee bits
½	cup coconut
1	cup raisins (optional)
½	cup dried cherries (optional)

Heat oven to 400° F.

In a large bowl, cream sugars and butter. Add eggs; mix well. Add vanilla. In a medium bowl, stir together baking powder, baking soda, salt, and flour. Add to sugar mixture. Mix well. Mix in oats. Add chocolate chips, toffee, coconut, and raisins and dried cherries, if desired. Drop by spoonfuls on an ungreased cookie sheet. Bake for 6 minutes, just until slightly golden.

Makes 7 dozen cookies

Save time: Freeze half of the cookie dough in this recipe for later use.

Sour cream makes these softer than traditional chocolate chip cookies.

2⅔	cups flour
1	teaspoon baking soda
½	teaspoon salt
1	cup butter, softened, cut in pieces
1	cup brown sugar
½	cup sugar
2	eggs
2	teaspoons vanilla
⅔	cup sour cream
1	package (12 ounces) semisweet or milk chocolate chips
1	cup chopped walnuts or pecans

In a medium bowl, stir together flour, baking soda, and salt.

In a large bowl, cream butter, brown sugar, and sugar until light and fluffy. Add eggs and vanilla and beat until well mixed. Mix in sour cream. Add flour mixture, and mix until just blended. Stir in chocolate chips and nuts. Chill dough for ½ hour.

Heat oven to 350° F.

Spray cookie sheets with nonstick cooking spray or line with parchment paper. Using a large spoon, mound about 2 tablespoons of dough for each cookie approximately 2 inches apart on cookie sheet. Keep remaining dough in refrigerator until needed.

Bake 12 to 15 minutes, until cookies are light brown and still soft. Rotating cookie sheets in oven halfway through baking will facilitate more even baking. Allow cookies to cool on sheets 5 minutes before removing to a wire rack.

Makes 3½ dozen cookies

STRAWBERRY TRIFLE

Make this glorious spring trifle when strawberries are at their peak. Try fresh, sliced peaches or raspberries for a satisfying summer trifle.

1	package (8 ounces) cream cheese, softened
1	cup powdered sugar
½	cup sour cream
¾	teaspoon vanilla, divided
½	cup heavy whipping cream
2	tablespoons sugar, divided
1	angel food cake (about 15 ounces), torn into bite-size pieces
4	cups sliced strawberries
1½	teaspoons almond extract

In a large bowl, thoroughly blend cream cheese, powdered sugar, sour cream, and ¼ teaspoon vanilla.

In a deep bowl, whip cream until soft peaks form; add ½ teaspoon vanilla and ½ tablespoon sugar. Fold into cream cheese mixture. Gently fold cake pieces into cream cheese mixture.

Put strawberries, 1½ tablespoons sugar, and almond extract in another bowl.

In a trifle dish or glass bowl, layer cream cheese and cake mixture, then strawberries. Repeat layers, ending with strawberries.

Serves 6 to 8

RASPBERRY DELIGHT

A light dessert to end a hearty meal. Try substituting strawberries for a different flavor.

FOR CRUST:

1	cup flour
½	cup butter, softened
¼	cup brown sugar
½	cup chopped pecans or walnuts

FOR FILLING:

¾	cup sugar
2	egg whites
2	tablespoons lemon juice
2	cups fresh raspberries or 1 package (10 ounces) frozen raspberries, thawed
1	cup whipping cream, whipped

Heat oven to 350° F.

In a medium bowl, mix flour, butter, brown sugar, and pecans or walnuts. Spread evenly over bottom of cookie sheet or jelly-roll pan. Bake for 10 to 15 minutes, stirring occasionally. Break apart and sprinkle ⅔ of crumbs in a 9- x 13-inch pan.

Put sugar, egg whites, and lemon juice in the bowl of a stand mixer. Whip at highest speed until frothy. Add raspberries. Continue whipping until stiff peaks form. Fold in whipped cream. Spread mixture on crust. Sprinkle with remaining crumbs. Cover and freeze for several hours or overnight. Soften slightly before serving.

Serves 9 to 12

BERRY FANTASY

Make this dessert with raspberries, strawberries, boysenberries, or blackberries—or a combination of them.

- 1 cup vanilla wafer crumbs, divided
- ½ cup butter, softened
- 1 egg
- 2 cups powdered sugar
- ½ pint whipping cream
- 3 tablespoons powdered sugar
- 2 cups berries, slightly crushed

Butter the bottom of an 8- or 9-inch square pan. Spread ½ cup vanilla wafer crumbs in pan. In a medium bowl, beat butter, egg, and 2 cups powdered sugar until smooth and spreadable. Spread mixture on crumbs. Sprinkle with ¼ cup crumbs. Whip cream and sweeten with 3 tablespoons powdered sugar. Fold berries gently into cream. Spread in pan. Sprinkle with remaining ¼ cup vanilla wafers. Chill. Cut into squares.

Serves 9

Family Tip: Start dinner conversation with the question, "Do you remember when?" and specify a particular enjoyable event or experience that the family can discuss.

PUMPKIN DESSERT

Serve warm with whipped cream on a cold winter's night to remind you of those glorious autumn days.

FOR CRUST:

1   package (18¼ ounces) yellow cake mix (reserve 1 cup)
½   cup butter or margarine, melted
1   egg, beaten

FOR FILLING:

1   can (16 ounces) pumpkin
2   eggs
⅔   cup evaporated milk
¾   cup sugar
1   teaspoon cinnamon

FOR TOPPING:

1   cup reserved cake mix
¼   cup sugar
1   teaspoon cinnamon
2   tablespoons butter or margarine, melted

To make crust, in a large bowl, combine cake mix, butter or margarine, and egg. Press mixture into a 9- x 13-inch pan that has been greased or sprayed with nonstick cooking spray.

To make filling, mix pumpkin, eggs, evaporated milk, sugar, and cinnamon. Pour over crust.

To make topping, combine reserved cake mix, sugar, cinnamon, and butter or margarine. Sprinkle over filling.

Heat oven to 400° F. Bake for 10 minutes, then reduce heat to 350° F and bake for 30 additional minutes (or until knife inserted in center comes out clean).

Serves 12

PINEAPPLE COCONUT PIE

A sweet taste of the tropics.

- 1 can (14 ounces) sweetened condensed milk
- 1 carton (8 ounces) Cool Whip, thawed
- 1 can (20 ounces) crushed pineapple, drained
- ⅓ cup lemon juice
- 2 (8-inch) graham cracker crusts
- 1 cup flaked coconut, toasted

In a large bowl, combine sweetened condensed milk and Cool Whip. Add pineapple and lemon juice, stirring until it begins to thicken. Pour into prepared pie crusts.

Place coconut on a cookie sheet and toast at 350° F for 2 to 3 minutes, watching closely so coconut does not burn. Or toast in microwave 2 to 2½ minutes on high. Cool and sprinkle over pie. Refrigerate several hours before serving.

Serves 10 to 12

Family Tip: If your family members' schedules conflict with dinner at an earlier hour, serve dinner late—maybe as late at 8:00 or 9:00 p.m. rather than skipping dinner or having everyone fend for themselves.

CRUSTLESS APPLE PIE

If you find making a piecrust from scratch to be a daunting task, make this pie without a crust!

4 to 5	large apples, peeled and sliced
1	tablespoon + 1 cup sugar
1	tablespoon cinnamon (or less)
½	cup butter, melted (or slightly less)
1	cup flour
¼	teaspoon salt
1	teaspoon baking powder
1	egg, beaten
1	cup chopped walnuts or pecans

Heat oven to 350° F.

Put apples in a 9-inch pie pan. Sprinkle with 1 tablespoon sugar and 1 tablespoon cinnamon.

In a medium bowl, mix together 1 cup sugar, flour, salt, baking powder, egg, and walnuts or pecans. Spread over apples. Bake for 45 minutes, or until golden brown.

Serves 6 to 8

CREAM CHEESE AND APPLE PIE

A very fine finish for any dinner.

FOR CRUST:

½   cup butter, softened
⅓   cup sugar
½   teaspoon vanilla
1   cup flour

FOR CREAM CHEESE FILLING:

1   package (8 ounces) cream cheese, softened
¼   cup sugar
1   egg
½   teaspoon vanilla

FOR APPLE TOPPING:

4   cups thinly sliced apples
1   teaspoon cinnamon
¼   cup sugar
3   tablespoons chopped pecans

Heat oven to 450° F.

Cream butter and sugar together in a medium bowl. Add vanilla. Add flour and mix well. Press into a 9-inch springform pan that has been greased or sprayed with nonstick cooking spray.

In a medium bowl, beat cream cheese and sugar together until well blended. Add egg and vanilla and mix well. Spread over top of crust.

Spread apples on top of filling. Combine cinnamon and sugar and sprinkle over apples. Top with pecans. Bake for 10 minutes. Reduce heat to 400° F and bake for 25 minutes. Cool before removing from pan.

Serves 6

VANILLA ICE CREAM

There's nothing like good old-fashioned homemade vanilla ice cream. Mix in fruit, candy pieces, or nuts for new flavors.

2	cups sugar
½	teaspoon salt
1	tablespoon vanilla
2	cups half-and-half
3	cups whipping cream
3	cups milk

Mix sugar, salt, vanilla, and half-and-half, stirring until sugar dissolves. Add cream. Transfer mixture to freezer container of an ice cream maker. Fill with milk to ⅔ full. Freeze as directed.

Makes about 3½ to 4 quarts

Family Tip: Have a banana split dessert bar for a special occasion. Serve homemade vanilla ice cream with bananas and let family members add their choice of toppings, including hot fudge, caramel, raspberry syrup, whipped cream, chopped nuts, candy sprinkles, and maraschino cherries.

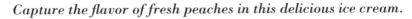

PEACH ICE CREAM

Capture the flavor of fresh peaches in this delicious ice cream.

6 to 8	large peaches, halved, pitted, and peeled
	Juice of 2 lemons
2	cups sugar (or to taste)
1	can (14 ounces) sweetened condensed milk
2	cups whipping cream
1	teaspoon vanilla
½	teaspoon almond flavoring
	Milk

Put peaches in a food processor or blender and process until nearly pureed, or mash with a potato masher. Put into a large bowl and add lemon juice and sugar. Refrigerate at least 2 hours. Stir in sweetened condensed milk, cream, vanilla, and almond flavoring. Pour into the canister of a 4-quart ice cream maker. Fill freezer container ⅔ full with milk. Freeze according to manufacturer's directions.

Makes 4 quarts

Save Time: Use a countertop ice cream freezer—it means no ice or salt and produces ice cream in about 20 minutes. It doesn't make a full batch, though, so cut most recipes in half.

ORANGE SHERBET

Experiment with other flavors of Jell-O and juices.

  1   package (3 ounces) orange Jell-O
  1   cup boiling water
1¼ cups sugar
  1   can (6 ounces) frozen orange juice concentrate, thawed
       Dash salt
  4   cups milk
  2   cups half-and-half or cream

Dissolve Jell-O in boiling water in a large bowl. Add sugar, orange juice, and salt. Stir until sugar is dissolved. Add milk and cream. Put mixture in freezer canister of an ice cream maker and freeze as directed.

Makes about 2 to 2½ quarts

RASPBERRY SHERBET

Light but satisfying.

  2   packages (10 ounces each) frozen raspberries, or 2½ cups
       fresh raspberries, slightly mashed
       Juice of 4 lemons
       Juice of 1 orange
  1   can (12 ounces) evaporated milk
       2 cups sugar
  ½   pint whipping cream
  2   quarts milk (approximately)
       Red food coloring (optional)

In a large bowl, combine raspberries, lemon juice, orange juice, evaporated milk, sugar, and whipping cream. Stir until sugar is dissolved. Pour into the container of an ice cream freezer. Add milk to the fill line. Add a few drops red food coloring, if desired. Freeze according to manufacturer's instructions.

Makes about 3 to 4 quarts

Contributors

Many thanks to the good cooks around the country whose recipes were tested, adapted, and enjoyed in preparation of this cookbook.

Myrle Adams
Peggy Andersen
Beverly Anderson
Rebecca Anderson
Sonia Aycock
Julie Black
Elizabeth Blaser
Pam Bleazard
Debi Brown
Anne Burt
Sue Burt
Sarah Burton
Betty Bybee
Stephanie Bywater
Amie Cannon
Gwen Cardall
Susie Cardall
Cindy Christensen
Patricia Cook
Lynda Cooper
Margo Cowley
Connie Crayk
Julie Crayk
Demetria Davis
Lorraine Day
Betty Draper
Janet Eggers

Linda Ellison
Jen Eyring
Rosemary Farmer
Suzanne Fjelsted
Kristen Fenn
Sue Ferguson
Nancy Flamm
Cammy Fuller
Marie Galbraith
Carol Gibson
Christine Gilbert
Sara Graham
Tana Graham
Cindy Grames
Devera Hagen
Dianna Hall
Sarah Harvey
Shauna Haycock
Natalie Heath
Paula Heath
Julie Hedman
Carol Horne
Stacie Hoyt
Kristen Hubbs
Nancy Hughes
Jen Judd
Tina Kargis

CONTRIBUTORS

Jane Kennedy
Joan Kimball
Amanda Laycock
Carol Larsen
LaRee Larsen
Margaret Larson
Kristen Lee
Connie Long
Cecily Mangum
Jan Martin
June Matheson
Lisa Matthews
Suzanne McAllister
Karen McCleery
Julie McDonald
Heather McGrady
Sylvia McRae
Pat Menlove
Anne Monroe
Eloise Morrison
Lenore Mott
Gertrude Muecke
Rebecca Nadauld
Christine Neilson
Debbie Nelson
Judith Nielson
Jen Oldroyd
Jessica Olsen
Krista Olson
Ann Painter
Jean Palmer
Christy Pando
Anna Peterson
Audrey Peterson

Kathy Jo Peterson
Lola Peterson
Sarah Plewe
Nola Porter
Teresa Powers
Sally Rasmussen
Marielle Rawle
Linda Ray
Kaylene Redd
Michele Reid
Tiffany Richards
Vera Richards
Camille Ricks
Wendy Robb
Shannon Robinson
Jan Rodney
Jen Romney
Sara Jayne Romney
Marianne Roy
Karen Sadler
Shelley Schenck
Heidi Shimmin
Judy Shimmin
Trudy Shipp
Maureen Shumway
Nahei Simpson
Nancy Simpson
Nancy Skaggs
Sheryl Snarr
Merrilee Soohoo
Allyson Sorensen
Elizabeth Sorensen
Jenn Sorensen
Jill Spencer

CONTRIBUTORS

Ann Spilker
Marie Stobbe
Jani Stone
Marcia Stosich
Penny Stratton
Marjorie Tall
Jennifer Tanaka
Jamie Tate
Dolores Montoya y Taylor
Brenda Thomas
Janiel Thomas
Marjorie Thueson
Barbara Townsend
Chris Tueller
Beth Udall
Brett Ure
Rebecca VandenAkker
Nancy VanSlooten
Joni Vincent
Susan Vollmer
Cinda Wade
Kathryn Wade
Shauna Wade
Eva Wallace
Kassie Warner
Tere Weir
Pat Wetzel
Ann Wittwer
Amber Wormell

Index

INDEX

INDEX

INDEX

INDEX

INDEX

Shepherds Pie -n- 102-103

INDEX